A Classful of

Gods & Goddesses

In NEPAL

A Classful of
Gods & Goddesses
In NEPAL

Ruth Higbie

THE BOXWOOD PRESS

PACIFIC GROVE, CALIFORNIA

Distributed by:

The Boxwood Press
183 Ocean View Blvd.
Pacific Grove, CA 93950
(408) 375-9110

Higbie, Ruth, 1909-
A classful of gods & goddesses in Nepal.

1. Peace Corps (U.S.)—Nepal. 2. Nepal-Description and travel. I. Title. II.
Title: Classful of gods and goddesses in Nepal.
HC60.5.H54   1988   361.2′6   88-6395
ISBN 0-940168-12-X

Printed in U.S.A.

Foreword

RUTH HIGBIE'S account of her Peace Corps experience in Nepal is significant on several levels. On one level, it is a charming, penetrating, and informative account of a beautiful land and a friendly people that American tourists are visiting in increasing numbers. Anyone who has been to Nepal and would like to know more about it, and anyone who plans to go to Nepal, or hopes to someday, should read it, for it will open their eyes to perspectives on the land and people that will greatly enrich their understanding and appreciation of that country.

Anyone concerned with promoting economic development and fostering international understanding in the Third World will find much of value in this book. They may not like what they find, if they are committed to one or another of the global theories of economic development that come and go with about the periodicity of fashions in clothing. For Ruth Higbie makes her friends in Banepa just as real for the reader as Steinbeck made the paisanos of Monterey. Inevitably and naturally, we come to understand that these people really aren't that simple, they think differently from us in profound ways, and "made in America" solutions to their problems can look just as unreasonable and even silly to them as their reactions to our "solutions" look to us. In my opinion that kind of perception is worth a hundred or so global theories for anyone who wants to understand what is actually going on in the Third World.

And yet, despite its bumbling nature and wrong assumptions, American and other Western aid *is* having an impact. Western ways of thinking are seeping in and finding their place in Nepalese views of the world, and a new generation is taking shape. Ruth's candid-camera snapshots of the people she lived and worked with vividly portray this many dimensioned process.

On yet another level, the book is a testament to the fact that however fat, ethnocentric, and self-satisfied we Americans may have become as we wallow in what promises to be our third generation of prosperity, we have not forgotten the rest of the world. At least not all of us. And some of us still retain the questing spirit and the curiosity about other lands and people that caused our immigrant ancestors to create the America we enjoy today. Ruth Higbie is one such American. She is modest and unassuming in private life, but also surprisingly perceptive and candid, and these qualities come through with pellucid clarity in her book. We end up knowing Ruth as well as we know the people she describes; her total experience becomes our experience. We share her sense of pride in what she has accomplished, and are reassured at the thought that her experience is being replicated by other Americans in many parts of the world.

I have strongly supported the Peace Corps program from its inception. I have recognized its importance in fostering good-will and implanting Western patterns at grass-roots levels in the Third World. But I have attached equal importance to the effect this program has had on individual Americans who have participated in it and, through them, on American society as a whole. It is a good program, and Ruth Higbie's book shows us why.

Carleton S. Coon, Jr.
American Ambassador to Nepal, 1981-1983
Washington, DC

An Appreciation

RUTH HIGBIE has written a beautiful book, a sad book, a joyous book. It is a book I wish I, an anthropologist, might have written. As a Peace Corps Volunteer courageously fulfilling a frustrating two-year assignment as a science teacher in a Nepalese village, Ruth was in fact a "participant observer" with her own role to play and therefore herself a thread in the colorful fabric she describes so well. Through Ruth's clear eyes and vivid writing we come to know her network of village friends and neighbors, her students and their teachers, and even a glimpse of her lone enemy, the "yelling man." The people of Banepa, her assigned village, are not simply statistical households, the "informants" of anthropological jargon, but real people with names, opinions, visions, and humanity. They are Gian Bhakta, the diffident little goat man, who cherishes his charges but for practical and spiritual reasons must sacrifice one to the gods. They are Krishna Maya, self-appointed mistress of the little courtyard of which Ruth and her by-Western-standards-miserable house were a part. And they are the matmaker's wife who by snatching away the shriveled potatoes Ruth thinks fitting only for the goats, tells us much about caste hierarchy and economics in Banepa. It is Ruth's friends, the Manandhars, who offer us a way to participate intimately in a Buddhist festival and we smile with her—and learn much about the Nepali family and even Nepali architecture—when, to make more room for the participants, they simply break a hole in the wall into the adjacent relative's house. Or finally, through the life of Ruth's neighbor, the lovely mute Om Devi, and the poignant death of her little son we learn about aspects of village life it would be hard to come by in the most fulsome anthropological treatise.

Unlike the American missionaries she thumbnail sketches so well in a chapter entitled, "The Intolerant God," Ruth understands that the profound cultural differences between her and her neighbors can be bridged, and has to be, if she is even to survive, let alone do the job she agreed to. When she realizes that flagrant cheating during exams is the accepted—and expected—practice in Ajad High School, and that she alone can't change it, Ruth solves the dilemma by boycotting the headmaster's farcical system of "invigilating." Intellectually, she knows that having a private toilet is contrary to Banepa practice, where the fields and alleyways have always sufficed, but with infinite patience—and a gentle ultimatum—gets the long-paid-for bricks into a wall around her outhouse.

Banepa, Ruth's home for two years that were "never dull . . . never easy," is one of some forty-odd, Newar villages that dot the Kathmandu Valley. Millennia-old, the villages are occupied almost exclusively by an indigenous population—the Newars— whose customs and language differ from the more recent, but now politically dominant, Nepali-speaking immigrants to the Valley. Through the magic of Ruth's pen and her accurate and sensitive observations as she went about her life, we too sojourn in such a village. With Ruth—but without getting *our* feet wet—we navigate monsoon Banepa "through the steady stream that flowed over the random stones and bricks of the bazaar street." We visualize the same "scrawny black hen trying to keep a pig away from her solitary chick," note the "wet crow [which] pecked at some manure," and splash along past shrines, and shops. By way of her own dwelling and those of her friends we are given a perfect description of the typical multi-story Newar house, its glassless windows, lack of running water, electricity, or sanitary conveniences, yet windows and doors often exquisitely decorated with carved wood and each house in harmony with its neighbors and with the land. We not only learn about the physical appearance and arrangement of a traditional Newar house but that the kitchen occupies the most impractical part of it—the top floor—because caste strictures so ordain. With Ruth we know also that the filth of a Newar village is more than balanced by the fascination of one. With her we waken pleasurably in her ascetic's bedroom to the sounds of neighboring Ganesh Lall's devotions, the gossip of crows, and the twitter of jungle sparrows. And with her we visit and worship at diverse shrines, Buddhist, Hindu, and animist, and share the excitement of the many festivals that punctuate the yearly cycle of a Newar community and the individual lives of her friends.

Life in Banepa for this newly-bereaved, middle-aged American suburban wife and mother, so suddenly a Peace Corps Volunteer in an alien world, was often "wrenching, depressing, and unbearable." But it was her love of the country, its people, and her gifted students that triumphed. If no others than the charming trio who daily descended to her classes from distant Wopi village, of which she writes so well, learned how to use their minds through her, sticking it out was worth the candle. That at the end of the two-year assigment, she was among only 19 survivors of the original 72 Nepal PCV trainees—most in their twenties, most given more agreeable surroundings, and most spared the trauma of coping with two difficult languages, Nepali and Newari—says it all. Courage in science teacher "Root, Sir" was obviously not in short supply.

Not only might an anthropologist envy Ruth's observations of Banepa and its surroundings, but also a naturalist. For though there was ugliness aplenty, Ruth was always able to see beyond, and describe both accurately and poetically, the splendor of the Himalayan rampart with its ever-changing palette of glorious color, ranging from pre-dawn jet to the crimson and blush of sunset. Chilly and lonely her house might be, but through the glassless windows she savored the evening flights of pearly egrets winging to roost. Or when she balanced precariously along the narrow dikes threading the flooded paddy fields, she did not dwell on the danger or discomfort but saw instead the "splashing frogs," the stalking egrets, and even a "black, red, gold, and chocolate grasshopper clinging to a dewy stem."

Throughout her two-year stay in Banepa, Ruth worried about her shortcomings in the Nepali language and the lack of Newari that perhaps more than any other factor kept her thinking that she was "adrift in a strange culture." But as I read this beautiful manuscript, it seems to me that early on and unawares Ruth had by her own strength and her own shining spirit, transcended the "strangeness" and fitted herself into that culture, successfully and productively, in a manner that is a credit to her, to the Peace Corps, and the American nation. I, for one, can't imagine anyone doing better.

Mary Shepherd Slusser

Acknowledgments

M Y BOOK OWES MUCH to the encouragement and search-light criticism of dear friends. I thank Berniece and Harry Neal and Elizabeth Olds who first said, "Oh, yes, go ahead with it." Dear Helen and Bill Avery, and Arabelle and Alexander Kossiakoff were wonderful and supportive critics. My son and daughter-in-law, James Higbie and Pamela Warfield, gave invaluable assistance in proofreading. Most of all I thank Carl Coon and Mary Slusser who went over the manuscript several times with the expertise and sensitivity of old-Nepal-hands.

To
the people of Banepa,
who will never know
how hard I tried.

Prologue

Mysterious Kathmandu

WE FIRST SAW KATHMANDU in 1963. Airplanes had begun to fly there only a few years earlier. Before that the only way in was by a perilous mountain trail. We heard of the place by accident; its valley was a green cup, lost in the Himalayas.

Roaming through Kathmandu and the two other cities of the valley, my husband Howard and I found nothing familiar. Temples with multi-tiered golden roofs were everywhere. In one of them, behind a door decorated with carved skulls, dwelt a Living Goddess. Tall ancient houses leaned together over narrow, roughly-cobbled streets.

City-scape of temples, palaces, and a gold king on a high pillar caught our imagination. This is part of the center of Patan, near neighbor and in ancient times deadly rival kingdom to Kathmandu.

Elaborately carved balconies and doors gave glimpses of brown-skinned women and girls in crimson saris with a dozen earrings in each ear, flowers in their hair, and red-stained fingers and toes. Men in something like *dhotis* and perky black fez-shaped hats, called *topis*, strolled the streets, or ran with yokes over their shoulders carrying double loads of huge shining brass jars, or buckets of water, or flat baskets of vegetables.

Newar farmer carries his baby as well as produce in baskets on a yoke.

Every step or so, we came upon a shrine heaped with flowers and daubed with red or yellow powder by worshipers. The gods these sacrifices were made to, amazed us. Beside a palace gate stood a figure so swathed in cloth and covered with red powder that we had no idea what it could represent. We saw devotees stoop to anoint with red powder a strange stone beast, or to place a garland around the neck of a cow.

Monks in orange robes strode silently through crowded alleyways. The people, of various shades of brown, were small

Children worshiping a fine ancient statue of Buddha. The boy places red powder on the Buddha's forehead. His little sister reaches up her offering of flowers.

Kathmandu

and handsome. Some faces were aquiline; some showed the slant of oriental eyes. Now and then we would hear bursts of music from drums and flutes. The hoarse blare of conch shells startled us. It was a jumble of images, sounds, and smells, all strange to us.

As dusk approached, flight after flight of white egrets winged in to roost. Together we watched their snowy, graceful forms silhouetted in startling beauty against the dark green forests of the nearer hills.

That evening, at the crumbling old palace where we were staying, one of the few guests said, "I have heard that for the festival tonight, sometimes they still catch a stranger and sacrifice him to the gods."

Answered Howard, "If you had told me that anywhere else in the world, I would have laughed."

A little apprehensively we went out to see. Flaring torches, small bands roaming the crowded streets, blaring and blasting. Incense in the air. Brilliantly colored and gilded idols. Little brown-skinned children smiling at us. Men in wild costumes dancing, whirling, and shouting. Color and lights shining in the darkness. Everyone laughing and excited. Two men dressed as monkeys with tails were having a duel with long heavy poles. People alternately crowded close, or screamed and tried to get out of their way as the "monkeys" dashed furiously at each other.

Women carried flower-heads, fruit, and rice to place before the images of gods. Men touched the offerings of red powder and marked their foreheads with it.

From the heavily carved window of one temple the images of a god and goddess leaned out to watch. Evidently the gods were as interested as the humans. We were caught up and swept along with the rejoicing, fervent people.

We could stay only three days, but of all the wonders we saw on a long round-the-world trip home from Hawaii, Kathmandu was the strangest, the most haunting to our imaginations. Even then it gripped my heart and I knew I must return someday.

Contents

1

Flight From Despair

I T WAS A SONG that drove me half-way around the world. Hearing it again at the moment I did was the final straw. Without it, I might have stayed on my Virginia farm forever.

There would have been no living in a village in Nepal. No mornings spent on a mountaintop to watch the sunrise over the Himalayas. No tiny sacred water-wheel made of a turnip. None of the joys or frustrations I found in a magic land under the snows. Those were not compensation for what I had lost: my husband and our way of life. But they were beautiful and exciting. More, they were the setting for my education in understanding a culture where "all the things everyone knows" aren't so.

What was the manner of my being wrenched loose? For over thirty years, life belonged to Howard and me. We had lived that many years together when we built a house on a hill facing the Blue Ridge Mountains, a house designed to watch the sunset over the mountains reflected in our own little lake.

At last the house was finished and we had one beautiful weekend there. For dinner on the terrace we ate bluegills we had just caught in our lake, salad from our weekend garden, and our own cantaloupes. It was a moment of contentment; we quietly watched the sky glow pink and orange and crimson, with the lake below it a bowl of flame opal.

Did he know his time was short? "There never was a day," he said, "that wouldn't have been better for 15 minutes more with you." Then, "This is a perfect evening. If we never had another all the trouble of building this new house would be justified now."

That was a Friday evening. Saturday morning Howard was

struck by a massive heart attack. In a month he was gone. I still cannot think of those days that were the end of our life together. After that I kept the house in town and the one in the country where we had been so happy. I tried to do alone the things we had done together.

In the end it was not the work that drove me away. It was pure desperation. I could not stand not having Howard. In spite of the mutual love and care my three sons shared with me, I found the days and nights insupportable. I tried for a year to endure in the places where we had lived so happily.

One night the radio played an old Tommy Dorsey record, a favorite of Howard's. It was *Marie, the Dawn is Breaking*, and it broke me. I ran wildly out into the dark along one of the farm roads until I fell down and sobbed in the damp grass. I lay there for an hour. When I got up I knew I must go away.

Where should I go? I had been writing about ancient shrines in the Mediterranean, but I shrank from the idea of cutting all ties and going off alone to a place where I knew no one. Perhaps Nepal, which Howard and I had been fascinated by? How would I live? Could I join the Peace Corps? Could I dust off my 30-year-old skill as a science teacher and sell that to them? I wrote for an application.

Then came qualms. Was I crazy? To think of going off as a Peace Corps Volunteer to teach in Nepal? I'd have to learn Nepali and teach in that Sanskrit-derived language. I'd never be able to do it. And Nepal was one of the most disease-ridden countries in the world. I'd take that instead of my farm in Virginia and my house in the Washington suburb, Bethesda? Live in a village without any frills like plumbing or sanitation or electricity?

Four years earlier, we had found it the strangest country in the world and the most remote from anything we knew. That must have been what drew me. If I was fleeing, I had better flee from everything. Most of my friends thought me demented. My sons said, "You can do it Mother." I wondered.

THE PHONE RANG. It was the Peace Corps. "Can you come to Davis, California on November 3 to join a group of volunteers training for Nepal? If that is too short notice, you may wait and join a later group of trainees." It was the afternoon of October 23, 1968, a Wednesday. I had two houses to dispose of, my husband's estate papers to get finished, everything to arrange for a two years' absence.

I gasped. "Would the later group be for Nepal?"

"No."

"I'll be there on the third."

In 20 hours the country house was closed up and in the hands of an agent, and I was in Washington for an interview with the Peace Corps.

The interviewer looked at my gray hair doubtfully and told me that there was a high attrition rate among older volunteers. In spite of his reluctance he allowed me to take the language aptitude test. When I passed, wheels began to turn.

I had already struggled with myself over the propriety of my going. I had no great feeling that I would be a boon to Nepal. I was supposed to be going to help the Nepalis change from their traditional rote learning to inductive reasoning. I told myself that everyone has a right to learn to think. But I remembered Nepal with its devout Hindu and Buddhist traditions, its marvelous and ferocious gods, its brilliant ancient religious festivals. I was forced to admit to myself that teaching people to think the way we do in the West might be the most mischievous thing one could do in such a culture. But I wanted to go. I said to myself, "Two governments are set on sending someone to Nepal to teach science. I will be more sympathetic to their values than anyone else. I must go."

The next evening a big Special Delivery envelope arrived. RUSH IMMEDIATE ACTION REQUIRED. I rushed. I filled out all the forms and had them in the corner mailbox by midnight.

That was Friday. Saturday, in Bethesda, I began to pack the

contents of seven rooms and fifteen years of occupancy. Monday I called movers and arranged about storage. They were to pack on Tuesday. I felt in a vortex. I tried to refuse all invitations, but agreed to a few farewell dinners. I'd be at home tonight and Tuesday night if anyone should want to say goodbye. On Monday about 30 people, and on Tuesday 40, were milling around among the packing boxes helping to reduce the contents of my cellar. On one box lay Toni Hagen's book on Nepal, with a picture on the cover of a mountain and a chasm. High up in the chasm two men with loaded baskets on their backs were crossing a badly broken bridge held together by a thin rope. My friends looked at it and shuddered.

In the middle of the party another special delivery envelope arrived. RUSH IMMEDIATE ACTION REQUIRED. Importantly, I opened it. I scanned the papers. They were all the same as the ones I had filled out Friday.

Saturday, after everything was packed, I received the list of things I must take with me. I had begged for it on Wednesday, but they wouldn't even read it to me over the phone. My name had not yet reached the proper desk. Now it was too late. I kept before me my shimmering vision of the brass-topped pagoda temples of Kathmandu. I gritted my teeth, and went to see the accountant who was working on the estate papers. I got my 1968 income tax form filled out as near as possible.

All this time, as I was signing Powers of Attorney, giving agents the right to rent my house for two years, paying for packing and storage, giving away quantities of food, I was realizing that I might bilge out of training and come crawling home, with Nepal farther away than ever.

On the plane west, the image of Toni Hagen's picture haunted me. There were shining mountains in the background. But what of the deep chasm above jagged rocks and the two puny humans crossing the dangerous bridge tied together at the splintered ends of an old break. Would those men carry their burdens safely across? Would I?

2

Training For Adventure
Will I Make It?

IN THE SACRAMENTO AIRPORT there was a group of bearded boys and long-haired girls. I felt foolish telling them I was a volunteer too. It was worse after we got to the Peace Corps Training Camp at Davis. I walked into an asphalt-shingled cabin where 10 girls were already sitting on their bunks. There was no other place to sit. They stared at me blankly for a moment, then recovered and greeted me politely. Too politely.

I got the last bunk—an upper, naturally. There was a shelf beside it, so I put my foot on that and climbed up. Someone offered to change with me, but I refused. To start being treated specially would be fatal.

The room had a cement floor, iron bunks, patched blankets. It was dirty. There were cobwebs in the corners. Outside there was mud everywhere, even on the cement sidewalks. Tar paper showed through asphalt shingles on some of the cabins. The electricity kept going off and on. There were two toilets for 90 people. I could see they were getting us ready for a life of hardship, but where did the University of California, Davis Branch, ever acquire such a pigsty? I found out it was once a bracero camp where migrant workers were housed. Poor migrant workers! We called it Cactus Corners.

My life had been soft. Now I must walk a block to the john, sleep in a saggy bunk within breathing distance of ten other women. I had one small shelf for my camera, typewriter, and all my clothes. I also had a moment of panic.

5

Then the girls began talking and I realized it was going to be pretty good after all. Alicia started. She was a big Italian, good humored, brash, and intelligent. She traded stories with Becky, a social worker, until everyone in the cabin began to feel at ease. Gloria, dark haired and shiny-eyed. Chris, a big blond with blue eyes and a cheerful smile. Jo Anne, with corn-colored curls. Donna was deselected (Peace Corpsese for dropped from the program) last year and was trying again. We also had a staff member, Patsy, and two of the Nepali language teachers, Azra, a Muslim, and Meera, a Hindu, like practically all Nepalis. Meera was married, her husband in Kathmandu.

There were 72 of us volunteers in camp including a retired teacher, Mary, who had more than my 58 years, and Harold, a man of 45. Nearly all the rest were 22 or 23. The girls were all from small little-known colleges. The boys (there were twice as many of them) were from Princeton, Yale, Stanford, Harvard.

The boys admitted and were bothered by the fact that their motives were clouded. Who could say they didn't volunteer for the Peace Corps to avoid the draft? In their conversations they worried the subject. Even the most idealistic felt that avoidance was in the back of his mind.

The staff was all young Returned Peace Corps Volunteers in love with Nepal and determined to help their charges with all difficulties. They tried so hard they almost lost their balance over the question of whether one could work in the Peace Corps of a government that was waging a war of which one violently disapproved.

Another question was how to deal with the problem of dope. Nepal's best cash crop is marijuana, *ganja*. The staff was frankly scared to death about the publicity that could be generated by one indiscreet volunteer. It could ruin the Peace Corps. However, in the climate of that time, they were afraid to issue a directive. In 1968, one must not be authoritarian. There would be a meeting to discuss it.

Tall, aggressive Ted wanted to know if this was the opening wedge, and what other liberties would be restricted? Mike asked what you could do if our director demanded actions we disapproved of. Could you write your Senators? Or the *New York Times*? Harold suggested we might work within the Peace Corps for change. Or, if anyone disapproved, the only honorable thing to do was to resign. "Don't give me that shit," shouted Ted.

Such language was still new to nice young people in 1968. Having me and Mary there to use it in front of was rather exciting. How they would shock us!

Middle-class was a pejorative to them. Being from the middle class, they thought that if they threw trash and garbage around, and said shit often enough, they would escape the middle class and their parents' influence. Such analyses I kept strictly to myself. I liked the volunteers. Some I became very fond of, though I couldn't say I ever felt that they could quite ignore my age. With Mary, the other gray-haired volunteer, I eventually became good friends, though throughout training I kept away from her. She wanted me to help her deplore the younger generation.

We arrived in Davis on Sunday. Monday we began to study Nepali. We all gathered in the one big classroom. In front a Nepali teacher stood and put her hands together. "*Namaste*," she said. Intelligently we put our hands in praying position and chorused, "*Namaste*."

Then she pointed to herself and said, "*Mero nam Kamala ho. Tapaico nam keho?*" and she pointed to one of us. After a lot of repetitions someone responded, "*Mero nam Mike.*" That was evidently not right. The question went on. "*Mero nam Kamala ho. Tapaico nam keho?*" Finally Scott jumped up and said, "*Mero nam Scot ho. Tapaico nam keho?*" "*Ramro, ramro,*" said Kamala, whose name obviously wasn't Kamalaho. We had learned four words, among them *ramro*, an invaluable term of approval. It means, good, wonderful, right, beautiful, almost anything pleasant you want it to. We broke up into groups of six to a teacher and gathered in corners of the cabins. Four symbols were on the blackboards.

क ख ग घ

Our first teacher was Dipendra, a strikingly handsome, neatly made, Nepali about five-feet-six. He pointed to the symbols in turn and said, "*Kuh, khuh, guh, ghuh.* We began what seemed by the end of the second week to be an endless flow of nonsense syllables. But nonsense or not, we couldn't say them right. We couldn't even hear them right. The aspirates escaped both our tongues and our ears. We said them wrong for an hour while Dipendra looked at us patiently with his large brown eyes, and began for the two-hundredth time, "Kuh, khuh, guh, ghuh."

With the 14 symbols for vowels and nasals and the 33 consonants, this went on for six hours a day in three sessions with a ten-minute rest every hour. This was varied by learning to count and eventually to make small conversational remarks. Strangely, sometimes at the end of two hours of frustration, one small part of the pattern came clear. Or a sound you could not make, emerged beautifully from your lips. A *djuh* properly aspirated, or a *tha* with the tongue in the exact right place— lips, tongue, teeth, and breath cooperating to make a sound the guru will call *ramro*!

Agriculture class served to relax the tension and, possibly, to teach us enough so we wouldn't be completely ignorant in a village of peasant farmers. We planted new hybrid varieties and might even learn enough to help the farmers. It seemed most unlikely to us. No matter. The rains came to Davis and the three-by-ten plots we planted began to sprout. We loved those little radishes in spite of our cynicism.

In Area Studies we looked at slides and talked about life in a Nepali village. The staffers talked knowledgeably about their villages and tried to give us an idea of what to expect. We acted out small dramas of village life. Some of us would be seven days' walk from the nearest transportation. I prayed that I wouldn't be that isolated, but none of us would have another volunteer in the same village. I began wanting to be in a village, not in Kathmandu. This was a surprise to me.

Sensitivity training was intended to make us more receptive to the emanations and cross currents in our villages. We had three psychologists in camp, and our director, Walter, seemed interested only in the sensitivity sessions. He gathered 25 of us into the big classroom. The floor was covered with mattresses. He spoke softly and soothingly. "Shut your eyes. Feel. Feel the way your feet meet the floor. Is it a friendly floor? Unfriendly? Let your consciousness explore your body. Let it flow up from your feet." Eyes still shut, we paused at our shoulders. "Lift them toward the ceiling. Relax. How do you feel now? Let your thought rise to your head, to the top of your head. How high is it? Is it close to the ground? Is it near the ceiling?"

We did quite a bit more of this kind of thing and then formed small groups to discuss reactions. Jim, the one black in the group, was much the most articulate and colorful in his reactions. Whirling stars. Great wells of feeling. He had trouble localizing the top of his head. He wanted his center of thought at the front, but it kept going to a spot at the back where he had a cowlick. Our group was through with talking and we broke up.

Leaving, Alicia and I were stopped by hearing Mike yell "shit." Then, "He is one of the most objectionable people I ever met!" He was talking about Ted, who had just said the whole evening was a puerile exercise in futility. The group jumped on Ted and continued arguing. Alicia and I left after awhile, but the next day we heard that the rest went on until one o'clock. Ted's opinion carried no weight. We continued to have sensitivity sessions, and a two-day encounter group at the end.

It had already been impressed on us that each of us would be "America" to his or her village.

After ten days of work, we had a day off. It was our first chance to leave camp. We had bicycles, but if we wanted to go far we were expected to hitchhike.

November 17 we changed language groups. A wrench after all our little group had been through together. I saw Ted in the dining room and said, "Oh, Ted, we are breaking a life-long association." "We'll have to have a class reunion," he answered.

Alicia was in my new group, and Scot, and Donna, and Bill. Every day we had several teachers in succession so we wouldn't get used to just one voice. Scot was very good, but kind to the rest of us. Alicia was good, too. Donna was ahead of us because of her former training. We were learning new symbols. Every time I learned one they gave me five more. I saw that I was going to be the slowest one in this group. Eight hours of language on some days. I wished for even more.

I was called away from dinner. A friend was on the line. None of my friends or my relatives could understand why I didn't have a private phone. What would they think of this place if they could see it? Would they believe that when I went away for a luxurious Thanksgiving vacation with friends I could hardly wait to get back to this frustrating language study? How could they understand the fascination it had for me, in spite of everything?

I couldn't find a spot on our littered grounds where I could sit and study without being surrounded by ugliness, so I cleared out a corner under a tree, found a more or less unbroken bench and draped some vines over the wall. Now it didn't offend me, and I could concentrate.

The group was dwindling. Becky, the girl I admired so the first night, was the first to go. She decided she would never learn the language. Then a boy went home to marry the girl he had left. After a few weeks, deselection began and several people were dropped. The rest of us trembled. I worked harder at Nepali, if that was possible. After an hour's intense concentration I sometimes dropped into bed and slept for the ten-minute break. A funny picture still remains in my mind—Ted stooping from his six-foot-five height to peer into little Dipendra's mouth to see how his tongue was placed. Was the "d" in *dhoka*

ड ट द   or   ध   ?

It was upsetting to the group when volunteers were deselected or decided that the Peace Corps was not for them. But at the end of three months there were 46 of us still there, having survived psychological screening, checks on what our friends at home thought of us and our habits, and the Foreign Service Institute Language Test. We had three days leave at home, and then met in New York for the flight to Nepal.

Before we went out to our villages, we were to have ten days in a Nepali home in Kathmandu. Alicia and I were to be together. After that we would all scatter to our unknown, frightening, lonely, demanding, and exciting jobs.

3

My Village

BANEPA lies 20 miles to the east of Kathmandu in the next mountain-locked valley. If I had come seven years earlier I would have had to walk eight hours to get there. Now there is the Chinese Road, and a bus from Kathmandu. At first glance Banepa seems a rather modern town with four- and five-story brick houses. The statue in the middle of the road might be King George if his crown weren't plumed with bird-of-paradise feathers. There was a jeep waiting near the statue. It all looked solid and familiar. At least, it looked so to me as I got off the bus that first day.

Five steps up the mud-and-cobble main street I began to change my mind. Hill women wearing red saris passed me, their gold-weighted heads bearing some 30 earrings and a couple of nose rings. The golden *tilari* of married women swung on the breasts of big-eyed girl children as well as wrinkled grandmothers. Merchants sat cross-legged on the floors of miniscule shops, smoking water-pipes and nodding to passing aquaintances with the tilt-headed nod of Nepal that serves for greeting, assent, thanks. One shopkeeper was wrapping a few *paisa* worth of spices in a green *sal* leaf for a shawl-swathed man. A bare-bottomed urchin drove three black goats.

The ring of metal on metal sounded. A goldsmith was rhythmically swinging his little hammer, beating out the links of an intricate chain. A single truck stood exhausted at a wide place in the road where a brick-enclosed pool and a temple to Ganesh mark the site of one of the old town gates. The truck had bumped over a third of the navigable road in Banepa, about 300 yards.

12

The wide area—I was to learn to call it Wokutol—was almost
filled with straw mats on which some seed I couldn't recognize
was drying. Over it sat women in bright saris, their waists
wrapped in thick layers of cloth. They were gossiping,
rearranging flowers in their hair, waving long bamboo poles
when a chicken or pig came too near the grain. A baby squatted
to defecate and a small black pig waited impatiently to eat the
fresh feces.

Three scrawny dogs spotted me and barked till someone
threw a stone at them. Everyone looked at me. A couple of little
children gave me *namaste*, their hands joined respectfully at
their foreheads. Beside them a group of ragged men squatted
over a card game beneath a beautifully carved wooden balcony.
A water buffalo poked his head out of a door.

I had arrived in Banepa, where I was to live for more than
two years. It is the principal bazaar town of a large and beautiful
valley. To the south the high green mountains of the
Mahabharat Lekh rise from their foothills. To the north the tall
forested hills are topped by the snow-and-ice mountains of the
Great Himalaya. In the valley between the *lekh* and the *himals*,
rivers wind through rolling plains. The scattered hills and
knolls are terraced as though a Master Artist could not be
content with the loveliest of contours, but must emphasize and
embellish them. Here and there nestle a few ochre-colored
houses of the new-come hill people, their thatched roofs curved
to let out smoke. Each one seems brushed in at the perfect spot.

The tall thickset brick houses of Banepa and a dozen smaller
towns cluster near the rivers. Above their tile roofs rise the
golden pagoda-tops of Newar Hindu temples. They shone
against the emerald terraces of winter wheat in January when I
first saw them. For many centuries the Newars of the valley had
worshiped in them.

These two kinds of settlements—the mud-and-thatch houses
in the hills, each sitting in its own terraced fields, and the

crowded brick-and-tile towns in the lowlands—are as different as their two kinds of inhabitants. Each has its own kind of beauty.

The land is lovely, whether lying mysterious in the mists of early morning, hard and clear in hot midday, or golden-green in the slanting light of later afternoon. Behind all is the godlike magnificence of the backdrop, the perpetual snows of the *himals*, whose outlines are seared into my memory.

From a small mountain across the river, I could call the roll of giants. Dhaulagiri, so far to the west that its 26,504 foot height is a small white mound against the sky. The bulk of Annapurna, Himalchuli's alabaster tower, and beside it Manaslu. The white wall lowers for a space, then breaks into the triple peaks of Ganesh Himal. And that is only the beginning of the fantastic foaming wave breaking across the northern horizon.

The names sing: Langtang, Gosainthan, Dorje Lakpa, Phurbi Chyachu, each with its distinctive shape. Choba Bhamare, Gauri Shankar, Cho Oyu, Nauptse, Sagarmatha—which foreigners call Everest—Lohtse, Makalu, Kachenjunga, and at the end of the line from my vantage point, the sharp pyramid of Numbur. They are the wall, the climax, the end of the world, where dwell the gods.

But the gods did not protect Banepa 200 years ago when Prithivi Narayan Shah came out of the west with his warriors. In those days the town was a Newari Princedom. It had a palace, and a tall Taleju Temple. It was walled with a high brick wall pierced by eight gates, each with its own ceremonial pool and temple to Ganesh, the elephant-headed god whose image is in every household, and whose three names begin the morning *puja*.

Now the palace is gone. The temple of Goddess Taleju is burned down. The stones from the walls are stolen. Grass grows from the roofs of temples, and the Newars have forgotten their ancient skills as wood-carvers and pagoda-builders. In the bazaar, only the goldsmiths still hammer out the old designs in huge earrings and golden headpieces for the women who come, with burdens on their backs, stepping barefoot along the steep trails from their mountain villages. They are the descendants of the conquerers, these hill people, but one would never guess it except that their Nepali speech is now the national language, while the difficult Tibeto-Burman tongue of the Newars is used in the bazaar.

The conquerors and the conquered dwell peaceably side by side. When the land belonged to the Newars, each tiny city state warred against its neighbors. That was more than two centuries ago. Now the country is unified and all profess a great veneration for their king, who is acknowledged to be an incarnation of Narayan (called Vishnu in India). Prithivi Narayan Shah's followers, who came down from the hills and have settled in the lower hills here, are Chetris, that is, of the warrior caste of Hindus, the same caste as the king himself, highest of all except the Brahman priestly caste. They wear the sacred thread of the twice-born, and no matter how simply and poorly they live, they are the superiors of all others.

The Newars, too, have castes. Some Newars are Hindu, some Buddhist, but their religious rites parallel each other, and there is no conflict between them. The gods are as tolerant as their subjects, sharing places of worship and festivals.

Temples and shrines are everywhere, and the people go out with offerings for them every day. Religious processions fill the streets with color, the glitter of gold, the sound of music. Some gods desire only flowers and vegetarian food, but others must have blood sacrifices. Chickens, goats, or water buffaloes are led to the priest to be sacrificed. Never pigs, unclean to most Nepalis, nor cows, sacred to all.

It was in this kaleidoscope, among these Newars of the town and Chetris of the hills, that I would live. They would be my students, colleagues, and neighbors. They and their country would come to be as memorable for me as they were for Toni Hagen, the Swiss geologist who was the pioneer mapper and explorer of the region. "After living here," he said, "the memory of Nepal will always remain with me like a star in the night."

But it wasn't going to be easy. That first day in Banepa I walked on up the rough cobbles carrying my suitcase and down sleeping bag and feeling very much alone in the teeming street.

Temple of Chandeshwari, Goddess of Banepa, in nearby hamlet, is a national place of pilgrimage.

4

My Newar House

T O REACH THE HOUSE that was to be mine, I passed
several shrines and a Buddhist temple complex. I turned
right down an alley and came to a sort of court. My house was
the first one, a tall dun-colored brick. I unlocked the double
doors and looked in. The ground floor was just that, ground. A
hallway led back to an empty stable. I regretted that I had no
water buffalo to put in it. At one side of the front door, stairs led
upward. They were like a ship's ladder except that as you put
your foot on it, each step wobbled.

The back room on the second floor was locked on some
stored goods of the landlord. The front room was mine. I
ducked my head as I entered. All the inside doors were four-and-
a-half-feet high. For the first week my head was a mass of sore
bumps. Then I found myself wincing and stooping whenever I
came to a doorway.

Two shuttered but glassless windows (there were no glass
windows in Banepa) reached almost to the mud floor. This is
not dirt but a surfacing of red ochre mud. Mud is what man is
meant to walk on. All the upper floors are carefully mudded
with red ochre and sacred cow dung to make a smooth, stucco-
like surface. Under this is several inches of white mud (which
Nepalis use for cement) on top of beams of dark *sal* wood and a
herringbone pattern of small pieces of wood. It makes a handsome ceiling for the room below, but gradually the clay sends
down drifts of dust. In this second floor room there were a few
books and some games for children, left by a former volunteer
in a small bookcase, the only piece of furniture in the house.

On the third floor there were three rooms: my bedroom,
sitting room, and "bath." The top floor was the kitchen. Newar
kitchens are sacred. They hold the family shrine. There the

17

sacred rituals of food preparation are performed. My large kitchen was directly under the tile roof. Smoke found its way out under the eaves. The slanting space between wall and roof formed the kitchen's only shelving. Outside in the eaves, pigeons made soft bubbling sounds.

A tiny clay stove was built into one corner. In another, a large square was paved and curbed with stone. That was my sink. A stone drain stuck out through the wall. In all the rooms my Peace Corps predecessor had left scattered debris of various kinds.

No electricity, no water, no cupboards, no glass window, no oven, no refrigerator. I looked about and began to think wildly: no dishwasher, no mixer, no disposal, no soft carpets, no tiled bathroom with gold spigots gushing hot and cold.

The last thought sent me rushing down those perilous stairs to find the *charpi*, the latrine I had been told was out back. From my unoccupied water-buffalo stall a double door let me into an eight-foot-square back yard. There had once been a wall between it and the street, but that had been broken down by many feet scrambling over it. The *charpi* was a small stick-and-bamboo shelter over an eastern toilet, which means a slab with footholds in front of a hole. The little hut had no door.

I was aghast. The *charpi* had evidently been invaded by the whole neighborhood, and the neighbors obviously didn't know how to use it; it was smeared and stinking. Thus suddenly appeared a basic confrontation between Nepal and me. This ridiculous *charpi* was to become a center of struggle and trauma.

I had the mud brick wall repaired and demanded a door for the little hut. I had the *piun* at school make a door of sticks and bamboo, but when attached it would not open—too little room between the hut and the back wall of the house. I tried making the door into a partition, tying it to a corner of the *charpi* and to one of the beam holes left in Newari houses. (Left so the rats can come in?) This closed my little yard off nicely. The neighbors broke it down.

I found—precious and unexpected trove—a great thick wire. With this I attached the partition again. It held for months. But someone started pulling pieces of bamboo out of the exposed wall of the *charpi*. I asked the girl who carried water to my kitchen to tell me who was taking my bamboo. She said she didn't need it. But someone did. The wall got thinner and thinner. I put a curtain on the inside. Next day that had disappeared.

One monsoon night I heard a great soughing collapse. I left my bed and went up to the kitchen. It was as usual; water was dripping musically into the 15 cans I had placed under 15 leaks in the roof. In the morning I looked out. My mud brick wall had slumped into the street.

Eventually I had a new, strong, baked brick, seven-foot-high wall completely enclosing yard and *charpi*. But that was only after I left my post and went off to Kathmandu saying, "Just send for me when you have finished the repairs I paid for three months ago."

I got my private *charpi*, but it was yielded to me as an idiosyncracy of my own. I didn't teach any Nepalis that they needed latrines. I smiled grimly to hear a missionary describe the streets as open sewers. A sewer implies some intention of getting rid of the offensive matter. In Banepa men went out to the fields. Women used one noisome lane reserved for them. Whatever was done by children lay on the steets until eaten by dogs or pigs, or picked up for fertilizer by a woman of the lowest caste who went around with two flat sticks and a basket. After I got it cleaned up, my *charpi* never smelled. It was blessed by an ever-flowing underground stream. Do not ask where the stream flowed to. I never dared to wonder.

This *charpi* problem took up too much time and emotion, as it has in my story. How can I explain that even in the most bothersome times I wouldn't have given up the chance to live just as I did in the midst of this strange town?

When I saw my own "instinctive" gut reaction in a place

where I was the only person reacting so, I had to realize my reactions were culture taught. So, when a Hindu, horror in his eyes and voice, asked me, "Do you eat cow?" I knew how he felt. I understood his own cultural abhorrence. His question was worse than "Are you a cannibal?" It was equivalent to "Do you eat your grandmother?" I know my reaction is right and reasonable. He knows his is.

I need my water boiled or germ-free. He needs his handed to him by a person of his own or higher caste. His precautions and mine have the same aim—to keep us free from pollution. And, having obeyed the rules of our own cultures, each of us feels secure.

But to go back to my first day in Banepa, which had only begun. The first arrival was Bishnu Maya, who had cooked for my predecessor. She was a pretty, round-faced peasant girl. She came to report to me and to guard the trash the last teacher had left as she abandoned her short and ill-fated career in Banepa. Over the protests of Bishnu Maya, I began to clear a space to lay my sleeping bag. Old letters, bobby pins, half-empty medicine bottles, papers—I had her sweep all of it into a basket for later burning.

She had left the door open when she came in. By now the house was full of tiny, bright-eyed Nepalis saying, "*Namaste Miss.*" "*Tapailai chaincha?*" (Do you need this?) as they picked up the things I was trying to throw away. All the small boys in the neighborhood seemed to have suddenly sprung up and to be running around "helping." To them it didn't seem strange that I had no furniture. They had none in their own homes. But my plans to burn trash distressed them. They carried it down to the yard for me, but even as I lit the fire, they grabbed things out of the blaze. Pencil stubs, ends of crayons, scraps of paper. "What do you want the paper for?" I asked. "To wrap things in," said these sons of merchants, who used their own copy books for spills to sell sugar in.

Upstairs again, I found more boys playing cards in the second-floor room. This had been an informal school once, and they knew where to find books, puzzles, crayons, and a game or two. I listened to their chatter and knew my Nepali was going to be inadequate. A tiny boy named Taro was winning the game. He smiled at me, his sculptured Mongol eyes nearly closing, his mouth stretched wide in the most engaging grin I had ever seen. Some of their faces were Mongoloid like Taro's, some Caucasian. Whatever the original inhabitants of the valley were, they had mixed long ago with Tibetans or Indians. I sat down on the floor with the children to watch the game.

"Do you go to school?" I asked Taro. My guess was that he was in the second grade. No, he was in the seventh and would be my pupil in the High School, which goes from sixth through tenth grade.

They all started urging a boy called Bhusan to dance for me. His smile, also, was captivating beneath his uncombed shock of hair. He wore a circlet of gold high up on his left ear. I would have guessed him to be in third grade, but he was another seventh grader.

The boys moved back against one wall and Bhusan got up. Feet patting and tapping, hands in stylized gestures, he did a Nepali dance for us. Bishnu Maya stood in the door to watch. A boy in shirt and pyjama pants caught up an empty coffee can and began beating out the rhythm. Bhusan, they told me, was by caste a dancer. His uncle was famous for his *lakhe* dance for which he wore a terrifying mask.

It was now four o'clock. Bishnu Maya told me she would start to cook my *bhat*. "No, Bishnu Maya, I want my dinner at seven o'clock, please."

"*Sakina.*" (I can't do it.)

"Why not?"

"Later going home, the leopards will eat me."

She lived in Chandeshwari about a mile across the rice

paddies. Leopards did kill pigs, dogs, or babies, and once in awhile a man or woman. She could not leave after dark. She would cook now and I could eat when I wished.

"No, thank you," I said. I already had hepatitis though I didn't know it yet. I only knew that *dal, bhat, tarkari*—lentils, rice, and vegetables highly spiced with *jira* (cumin)—stuck like a baseball in my chest. I couldn't face it cold.

"If you want me to cook later, I can stay all night and sleep in your bed with you."

"No thank you."

"*Ekle basne, ramro chaina* (to live alone is not good)," said Taro. But before I could express myself on what was always to be a controversial subject, we all raised our heads to listen.

There was a beat of drums and approaching music. The boys scrambled to their feet. "*Aunuhos*," said Bhusan. In the hall we paused to slip into our shoes. Bishnu Maya, not burdened by shoes, was ahead of us. We ran down the narrow lane into the bazaar some 60 feet from my door. The drums were passing loudly, behind were keening wood instruments, then a man whose instrument was a row of small cymbals on a stick played with a broad sweeping motion of the arm. "That's all," said Taro, "They are going to the temple at Chandeshwari."

I gave Bishnu Maya some money and told her to buy me bread, butter, eggs, sugar, salt, milk, some kind of vegetable, and some meat. She started voluble protest, but I walked off firmly. In half an hour she came back with two eggs, a quarter cup of sugar twisted in paper, two small potatoes, two onions, four bananas the size of my thumb, and some gray lumps.

I sputtered, but had to listen this time. In Banepa there was no bread. Never? Never! No butter? Again, never; ghee was available, but no butter. Potatoes and onions were the only vegetables available in the bazaar today. As for salt, from the corner of the kitchen she brought out a stone mortar and another stone to pound the gray lumps with. Salt, see! Also she

had bought rice and spices. I must have forgotten to mention
them. She counted out my change. She had spent 23 cents. Now
it was time to go. Soon it would be dark and the leopards would
eat her if she didn't hurry.

I barred the door behind her and all the little boys. I made
myself an omelet on a tiny one-burner kerosene stove I had
brought with me. I boiled the potatoes in a broken pot, and
seasoned them with gray salt. The tiny bananas were dessert.

It was evening and the chill air began to suck up all the
warmth my body could muster. I crawled into my sleeping bag,
intending to think about the day. But a sudden spasm gripped
me. Oh Howard, my love, where are you?

The sound of music going through the bazaar was frequent. Here the
Nanandhar caste musicians return from worship at Chandeshwari.

5

Eschool

SINCE five o'clock that morning I had been desperately trying to fix and refix in my mind the Nepali words I needed for my first science class. It was February 8, 1969, the first day of school in Ajad High School. I had been learning Nepali for only three months and had passed the Foreign Service Exam with a 1+ which means something like, "can barely get along in the language." My head was crammed now with wiggly symbols and innumerable strange sounds that my tongue and throat could not accurately make.

It was the first day of the school year, and, for me, the first day of teaching in some 30 years. I was the only woman on the faculty, and the only teacher who was not a Nepali. I was desperately scared.

I could feel myself trembling inwardly as I walked the mile up hill to the school perched above the once noble town of Banepa. The shrines and temples along the way, the children calling respectful *namastes*, all were a blur to me. Only where the path opened on a glimpse of the fluted snow tower of Himal Chuli against the blue sky, did I take a little heart from its beauty. Though I didn't know its name yet, it lifted my spirits and I kept my face toward it as I climbed the rest of the way to the school.

No one was in sight. I looked at my watch. Yes, it was ten o'clock, the hour at which schools open (government offices too), allowing time for morning worship and the sacred first meal of the day at home. I sat down, not at all sad that I couldn't begin at once. I'd have liked to delay that first class forever.

The school is a handsome ell-shaped structure of rose colored brick built around what must have been intended for a pool, but was a dry mud hole. I sat down on the edge of the arcaded porch, which ran all along the inside of the ell. I faced south, toward

24

the Mahabharat Lekh, the high green mountains that form the southern rampart, keeping Nepal a closed and secret kingdom for centuries. Rivers wind between scattered villages on their way to a gap in the Lekh. The green hills are terraced and cultivated. In the near foreground below me lay Banepa. Tall brick houses close together, punctuated here and there by the brass pagoda top of a temple.

After 20 minutes of looking at the view I saw two boys coming along the dikes between the rice paddies below. They wore *topis*, the perky Nepali hats, one black, one *rungi-chungi* or multicolored. Though it was so cold that I wore a wool suit, they had on cotton shirts open at the neck. The boy with the *rungi-chungi topi* had bare feet and shorts almost covered by his hanging shirt. The other had striped pyjama pants and tennis shoes.

When they reached the school they gave me a shy *namaste* and started to go farther along the arcade. *"Timro nam ke ho?"* I asked. They told me their names were Janak Bahadur Thapa and Yegya Bahadur Thapa. *"Daju bhai?"* Yes, they were brothers, meaning, in this case, cousins.

Ajad High School where the author taught science for two years. Houses of hill people are scattered above.

"Where is everyone?"

"They will be along later."

"But it's time for school."

"Yes, it is late," they said and sat down to wait.

After a minute, I said, "Where are your homes?" "*Mati*," they waved at the green mountain to the northeast. "How long did it take to walk to school?" "About an hour." "Isn't it hard to come that far every day?"

"No. School is very important." They used the English word, but pronounced it "Eschool." "We like to come. We were the first students ever to come to the high school from our village, Wopi."

Their smiles came and went, lighting their faces with intelligence and interest. I didn't know it yet, but I had just met two of my best students.

Two of my best pupils, Yegya Bahadur Thapa and Janak Bahadur Thapa.

"Headmaster *ayio*," said Janak, and I saw Ram Bhakta, whom I had already met, coming up the path beside a tall man with a small round head. Both wore Western suits but no neckties, black *topis*, and the pointed black leather shoes modern Nepalis affected. The second man was Asha Kaji, Assistant Headmaster, and the only teacher beside Ram Bhakta who had a Master's degree. "*Thulo mancheharu* (important men)," said Janak.

Gradually 12 teachers and 380 pupils assembled, 80 of them girls. The other teachers were dressed like Ram Bhakta and Asha Kaji, or in the national dress that consists of *suruwal*, cotton pants of loose fit in the seat, tight in the legs, and a matching fitted long coat with a shorter Western suit coat over it. And of course, *topis*, usually black.

Most of the boys were dressed like Janak and Yegya. A few of the wealthiest ones wore Western suits. All had one or two small gold circlets in their ears, either in the lobe or high up toward the top of the ear. All the teachers had pierced ears, but none wore earrings. They were too modern and enlightened.

Girls wore *suruwal* pants with a long blouse or short dress over them and a long scarf, the color of the *suruwal*, thrown gracefully over the shoulders. In their hair they wore flowers and in their ears one pair of earrings—in contrast to the older women, who often wore a dozen or more to an ear. None wore a nose ring, though a nose stud was worn by the low-caste girl who helped her mother carry water up to the school from the village. This girl wore a sari instead of the costume worn by all the school girls. They would put on saris when they married.

They were an attractive lot, both boys and girls, smooth creamy brown skin, clear eyes, a fine smile, and a red *tika* mark on the forehead from the morning worship.

I need not have worried about teaching that day, or the next, or the next. Gopal Man, the handsome teacher/treasurer with the classic profile, sat at a table in a window of the teachers'

Girls of Ajad High School.

Eighth science class, Ajad High School.

room. Children beseiged him from inside the room and outside
on the grass. Waving money in their hands, they clamored to
register and pay their fees. It cost ten *paisa* (one cent) for the
registration blank. The fee for sixth grade was $1.95 for the
first month and 90 cents per month for the rest of the year. Fees
were higher, grade by grade, up to $2.75 a month for tenth
grade. Between the cost of those fees and the lost labor of the
child in school, it was expensive enough that hardly any but
well-to-do families sent a child to school.

The first questions on the registration form were name?
religion? caste? Our children were nearly all Newars from
Banepa and the smaller Newar towns of the valley. Of these a
third were Buddhist, two-thirds Hindu. From a few scattered
hill villages like Wopi came Hindu Brahman and Chetri boys,
that is, those of priestly or warrior caste, none from the lower
castes. Two untouchable boys from Banepa had government
scholarships. There was no hostility to them, but none of the
children associated with them.

The first few days of school were devoted to milling around,
copying the schedule posted in a locked metal grill, recopying
the changed schedule that took its place next morning, and the
further changes that afternoon.

We sat on the arcade in the sun on chairs the *piun* brought
out for the teachers. The students stood in clumps and looked at
us or leaned over our shoulders if we read or wrote. I listened to
the talk. To my distress the teachers talked to each other almost
exclusively in Newari, though all classes by law must be taught
in Nepali. How would I ever learn Nepali if they didn't speak
it? If I couldn't learn from listening?

Prithivi Narayan Shah may have conquered in 1768 and
imposed the Nepali language on the country, but the Newars
clung to their difficult, ancient Newari. That was the language
the children learned on their mothers' backs. In our school all
the teachers were Newars, and that was what they spoke

between themselves by choice. In hill villages like Wopi, Nepali was spoken. That gave Chetri children a head start in the high school, where all classes were supposed to be taught in Nepali.

Surrounded by an incomprehensible babble of Newari, I felt strange and isolated. Until the end of my stay I would sometimes feel so. I never tried to learn Newari; I had to bend all my strength toward getting Nepali into my head. And even when that language came easier and I could understand the words, I could never be sure I got the nuances, the real intended meaning.

I must have presented a problem to my Nepali colleagues. Ram Bhakta was always friendly and helpful, and two of the other teachers became my friends. One was Jnan Kaji Manandhar, who taught English in the high school and was Headmaster of the Morning School that met in our building at 6 a.m., the Nepali version of night school. After these morning classes he went home for breakfast and worship. He gave me the impression that he had a Master's degree but it wasn't quite true. His pride was that he had gotten far enough to take the exam for M.A. even though he failed it. That was more education than anyone else in the whole valley had had except Ram Bhakta and Asha Kaji.

My other friend among the teachers was Krishna Prasad Duvall. He had taught a dozen years without ever having passed the School Leaving Certificate (SLC) exam, which comes at the end of tenth grade. Yet he was a poet with two books published in both Nepali and Newari and he was a man of intellectual curiosity willing to defy convention. He would come to my house and talk for hours. His kitchen was one of the only two I ever entered in a Nepali house. He and his wife were unconventional enough to invite me in. Though I was often invited to eat a *bhoj*, I was always served in another room in every other house I visited except Ram Bhakta's and he had been to the United States, thereby becoming unconventional himself.

Three of the teachers had two wives. Two kept separate establishments for each wife and her children, but Gobinda could not afford that, so his double family all lived together. Though he was about 49, he had an impish smile and I liked to think they all had a good time together.

The mathematics teacher lived in a big house with the most beautifully carved windows and balconies in Banepa. His extended family of 35—brothers, sisters, uncles, and aunts, and their children—lived there also. I worried about them because a three-inch crack ran jaggedly down one corner between the bricks.

The only Brahman on the faculty was Kedar Nath. He lived in a rented room in a nearby Brahman hill village in preference to Newar Banepa though he had to walk an extra mile before starting the climb up to the school.

The school building looked fine from the outside. It wasn't a skimpy lean-to such as some towns had. Our arcaded brick building was impressive until you stepped into a classroom. The floors were dirt. There was no glass, no electricity, and when the shutters were closed, no light. In monsoon season the roof leaked and produced ponds in the middle of some classrooms, and the children had to squeeze against the walls.

They sat on benches and had higher benches about 11 inches wide to use for desks. Girls always sat on the right of the center aisle, and boys on the left. There were always more boys than girls, so the extras sat at the back behind the girls, leaving as big a space as possible. The number of small Nepalis who could crowd onto a bench was amazing. They sat entwined, sharing books, papers, and thoughts.

There was a small room called the library, with a few dusty books and magazines on flimsy shelves; but no one was allowed to read them. The "library" doubled as a ping pong room, as UNESCO had given Ajad High School a ping pong set. A game on the dirt floor raised thick clouds of dust that smothered every surface in the room. The school floors were not mudded, but were simply dirt. The red ochre mud and dung coating used in our houses was much too fragile to be used here.

I became familiar with that layer of dust because my tenth grade optional biology class often met in the "library." That is, it did when the key could be found. Then in October a wild streak of vandalism struck and the furniture in that room started to disintegrate. Legs disappeared from benches and tables until there was no place to put 20 children, and we would have to go outdoors on the grass, not the best place to work on diagrams they were going to need to know for the national SLC exam.

Three periodicals came to the school. The USIS magazine was printed in Nepali and had articles evenly divided between Nepal and the United States. The other two magazines were bigger and thicker and glossier, one from China, one from North Korea. Both were written in English, and they single-mindedly sang the glories of communism and the dedication of its workers. The United States was frequently cited, never without a pejorative. It stood for everything bad and wicked in contrast to China and North Korea. This simple heavy-handed approach is probably effective with people whose ability to read English is minimal. There were many bright glossy illustrations, and the paper was thick.

The magazines were highly prized for a special use. Nepalis love to go on picnics, and I would often take a class on a picnic to the top of some small nearby mountain. They always begged to take along the Chinese magazine. It made paper plates far superior in their minds to the traditional glossy green *sal* leaves.

Communist books as well as magazines had a wide distribution. The Communist Book Store was a cubbyhole up at Tin Dhara, the open "square" above Wokutol. It was much pleasanter than the other book store. If I went in, the proprietor rushed to dust off a bench for me and made me welcome, though I was the United States representative in Banepa. For half a cent you could buy *The Thoughts of Chairman Mao* in a two-inch, red plastic-covered volume and a matching one, *The Constitution of Communist China.* Many of my students wore the little red books in their shirt pockets, but I am sure no one ever read them. All the communist books were very cheap, and they were almost the only books I saw in anyone's house.

As well as the "library," the school had a closet grandly called "the science laboratory" where equipment was kept. Ajad High School was fortunate in having a microscope, a few beakers, test tubes, an alcohol lamp, magnets, prisms, and some chemicals. Most were gifts from UNESCO. The microscope was a present from a high school in California that Ram Bhakta had visited when he was in the United States on a fellowship three years earlier. Another high school in the same town had been so impressed by Ram Bhakta's stories that teachers and pupils had worked for months to put on a big fair to raise money for Ajad. This, Ram Bhakta told me, was to be used to build a real science laboratory. Of course the school had no water or electricity, though there was a derelict half-finished reservoir. The nearest electricity was in Banepa, a mile downhill.

Ram Bhakta said the science laboratory was to be started in the next two months so as to be under roof before the monsoon season in June. I would have a fine place to teach, he said. I hadn't been in Nepal long, but somehow I didn't count on that laboratory. Its final history was a sad one and could have been instructive, but the message it might have given was lost in a mist of misunderstanding never to be resolved in my time.

6

A Classful of Gods and Goddesses

CLASSES did finally start and I could no longer put off that first lesson which I so dreaded. As I entered the door to the sixth grade class a solid roomful of small Nepalis jumped to their feet and chorused "*Namaste.*" It was their first high school class, and they looked frightened too. The muscles of my face relaxed enough to let me smile, and the room rippled with timid grins. "*Namaste*," I said. "*Basa.*" They sat.

A hundred and thirty dark eyes fixed me. Some were round, some slanted, reflecting the mixed origins of Nepal from southern plains and northern mountains. I had to gulp twice before I could introduce myself. "*Mero nam* Mrs. Higbie *ho*," I said, writing it on the blackboard in English and Nepali script. "Misiz Higbie," I said, and "Masus Hagbi," they answered. It was a difficult name for them and I was seldom called by it. Masus, Master, Miss, Root, and sometimes Root Sir. The English *th* is an impossible sound for a Nepali. The only thing I wouldn't answer to was the grunt "*Eh*," which wasn't as impolite in Nepali as it sounded to me.

As for their names—it was a classful of gods and goddesses. To my roll call a heavenly chorus responded. Krishna, Shiva, Ganesh, Laxmi, Indra, Gunga Devi. There was one Western god—that malignant demon Hitler. I jumped when I saw that name, and wondered how in the world he got there.

34

My panic about teaching in Nepali hadn't abated much in the days of respite. I knew my accent was strange. My 58-year-old tongue couldn't make all the sounds; my ears couldn't even distinguish them. There are in the Devonagri syllabary in which Nepali is written four *t*'s, four *d*'s, two *k*'s, two *g*'s, and so forth and so forth. To complicate things still further most of the children had been taught their lessons in Newari for the first few grades, and it was the language spoken in their homes. Between us we had more than enough language problems.

One of the pitfalls of a strange tongue is that differences in sound that don't matter in your own language, do take on an importance in the new one. Nepalis don't make the same distinction we do between *s* and *sh*, so in their mouths, for instance, the English sentence "Won't you please sit in the chair?" dropped innocently into a conversation can turn into a social disaster.

In Banepa's mixture of Nepali and Newari exactly the same mistake is possible. There are two *k*s; one is aspirated and transliterated in English as *kh*. The difference between *kh* and *k* is easy to make. It isn't like one of the *t*'s and one of the *d*'s, which require you to double your tongue back against the roof of your mouth, a feat I found almost impossible to accomplish in the middle of a word without bringing the whole sentence to a complete halt while I contorted my tongue. *K* and *kh* are easy, but since the difference isn't important in English, it is also easy to use the wrong one, especially if you are being emphatic.

Now a science teacher trying to get a class to think uses one word frequently and with fervor—why. The sun appears to rise in the east. Why? The north star seems to stand still. Why? There are no frogs in the rice paddies in the coldest month. Why not? The word for why is *kina*. I was always using it, emphasizing it in hope, exasperation, and despair. Sometimes I'd hear muffled giggles from the back of the room. Sometimes even my best pupils would smile and look at each other for no reason I could see. I went innocently on. Until one day one of the teachers spoke. He was not a special friend of mine, for evidently this was the kind of thing your best friend won't tell you. "Root, *kina* in Nepali means why, but you often say *khina*." "And what does that mean?" "In Newari it means human excrement." If Shiva could have danced his dance of destruction and brought the world to an end right then I would have rejoiced.

My classes would stare at me as I labored to communicate. My odd accent, the strange ideas I was bringing from the outside world, the unfamiliar concepts and methods—all were difficult and bewildering. Their traditional way of learning was to memorize. I was there to help them understand. But surely those first classes of mine must have been among the least understood of all time. I suffered over every mistake.

The mistakes the kids made in English often charmed me. There was the note signed Your Lovely Students. And the little boy's English Exercise Book which began in print:

> He does, doesn't he?
> He can, can't he?
> He is, isn't he?

And continued in his writing:

> He swims, swim't he?
> He jumps, jump't he?
> He runs, run't he?

As my language improved and the students got used to me we drew together, but then I began to see the deep gulf that yawned between these children and the type of education His Majesty's Government had decided it wanted to give them. It was only in the last few years since King Tribhuvan had thrown off the paralyzing rule of the Rana Prime Ministers in 1951, that there were schools at all. None of the mothers or fathers of these children had been to school and only 2% of the men in Banepa claimed to be literate. Hardly anyone saw school as much more than a prestigious activity, generally useful in raising you above the necessity of work, not teaching you how to perform it. It certainly didn't take precedence over the religious festivals which occurred every few days and often lasted for weeks. These were of vital family and cultural importance.

And the educational system was ill fitted to help the students. The British schools of India had been the model, and they in turn had been patterned on the schools of England of an earlier day. I found that in English class they studied poems my mother had memorized before the turn of the century. It was strongly laced with the tradition of a guru whose words the students repeated in unison as they sat on the floor around him.

The textbooks. Oh, the textbooks! They were thin and small with soft paper covers. Every author believed that the more long words he could cram in the better. His prestige would soar if he were too erudite to be understood. The Biology text contained hundreds of terms an American college student wouldn't know. Yet these ninth and tenth graders, new to any kind of scientific terminology, were supposed to remember epiblems, peristomium, chondriosome, ergastic substance, hercogamy, theistogamy, and a hundred others for the vital big SLC exam without which a government job or further education was impossible.

The texts were full of a bewildering variety of misprints and errors, often indistinguishable. The ank of the frog, the hem of the plant, the auld of the insect. What was a child who knew little English to make of these? The text was in Nepali, the diagrams supposedly in English. Here was another dilemma for me. If I corrected the texts would the examiner know the right answer, or would he hold to the text? Was I dooming my pupils to failure by teaching them the facts?

There were erudite words and constructions borrowed from Sanskrit that were in none of my five dictionaries, and that none of the teachers or even the Headmaster could understand and translate for me.

The courses had no logical organization. If one is only trying to memorize a body of facts and not trying to make sense of them it matters not at all in what order they are learned. Under the old gurus one listened and remembered. For some levels of instruction one didn't even have to be able to read.

At least my classes could read. Not silently. No one read silently. Classes chanted their lessons; teachers in the office read newspapers aloud to themselves. The sixth grade could read with a speed and authority that I envied. I still had to puzzle out the Devonagri symbols. They didn't automatically say themselves as a glimpsed English sign does. For my children, they did. They came out in the correct sounds. But that was all. When I asked questions about what they had just read so glibly they stared at me.

They read:

> Our sun is one of the stars, not a very big one,
> but it is the closest of all the stars to our earth.
> That is why it looks much bigger and brighter
> than the other stars.

"Shiva Prasad," I'd ask. "What star is closest to the earth?"

Shiva Prasad would stand. Agonized, he would look around the room while his classmates stared back at him.

"What did the book say, Shiva Prasad? Is there a star close to our earth?"

"The North Star?"

"No, another one."

"I don't know the name of another star."

"What did you just read in the book?"

Silence. "Who does know?"

After more minutes of questioning and rereading, someone would say "the sun." When they had gotten used to the strange fact that I would ask questions, the pattern was different. There were always two or three, rarely more to a class, who always had the answer and tried to respond to every question. To draw out the others was impossible. From shyness, confusion, or lack of understanding, they were mute.

I gave multiple choice tests—choose between four possible answers. They had never encountered anything but essay tests before. Still, by the blindest of blind guessing they should have averaged 25%. Their scores were abysmal. We would go over the test in class, practice the same questions and repeat the test. Even after that some classes averaged 18% or 20%. A passing grade at Ajad High School was 35% and I did want *some* of them to pass. Many didn't really expect to. They could fail in two subjects and still pass to the next grade. A lot of tenth graders had never passed English or math.

In the end I taught for the few children who were trying to learn, though even they would not do homework. Our school was not unusual. I heard the same story from teachers in other schools around the country.

7

One Day at Ajad High School

ONE JULY MORNING recorded in my notes gives a picture of my school day:

Before five o'clock the crows begin to caw. I push out of my mosquito net, descend three flights of stairs, unbar the back door and go out in the still-dim light to my latrine. On the way back I unlock the front door (having relocked the back one) so Om Bahadur, my present cook, can get in. While he heats water for my bath he goes out to get goat meat for dinner (it is available only for a few minutes at a certain street corner where the butcher who killed and prepared it last night will squat with his scales to weigh the meat and wrap it in green *sal* leaves). Meanwhile, I sit on the cushion by the front window to work on the day's lessons.

Om Bahadur brings me my coffee, and I order scrambled eggs, fresh-made potato chips, and a banana mango compote. I go on planning. He brings a large brass basin full of hot water to my "bathroom" and I stop to take a sponge bath. Between bath and breakfast I put my lessons into Nepali.

At a quarter to ten I leave, carrying paper for a test, chalk, eraser, a cardboard box for an experiment, a potato, an umbrella (this is monsoon season), and keys for the pitiful library and laboratory. On the path up to school I pick a supply of leaves, monocot and dicot, bamboo and hibiscus for a class of 63, stowing them with the rest of my equipment in my *jhola*, or shoulder bag. Two men in *dhotis* appear and watch me. I tell them the leaves are for my biology class. They help me reach some high ones.

When I go on, one of the men, a musician with a crude violin-like instrument, walks with me and to my surprise tries a few words of English.

This day I don't have a class until second period. At school a few teachers have arrived and are sitting in the arcade. We *namaste* each other, our hands folded together. No one seems to be teaching though it is ten minutes past time for classes. I had brought a couple of *Time* magazines. Issor Bhakta and Gobinda take them and start intoning the captions under the pictures to themselves. Most of the teachers have a few days' beard but manage to look fairly neat. Maybe bristle looks worse on a white skin? Or maybe I can't remember what a well-groomed man looks like. I go back to the office for a table on which to draw a series of large colored diagrams showing how a bee fertilizes a flower. First a whole flower, then cross sections showing all the parts of the flower with the bee going in and out. In class we have been trying to get the idea of what a cross-section is by cutting stems and various objects. The maps and diagrams Westerners take for granted are strange and incomprehensible to people who have never seen them before. Our "instinctive" understanding comes from long familiarity with them.

The *piun* comes out and rings his handbell for second period. I notice that by my watch it is ten minutes late. Krishna Prasad and Kedar Nath continue their chess game. Rajendra keeps on reading. The rest sit still. I get up and walk slowly toward the seventh grade classroom giving the kids time to stream in in front of me as the word is called out that the Science Master is coming. I have my books, umbrella, chalk, etc., but there is no table to put them on. I reach over the heads of three little girls and lay them on the dusty window ledge. The box, and a potato to sprout in it, are for this class, and I ask three children to put their books in their laps so there will be room on the narrow high bench in front of them for our experiment.

It is to show how light affects plants. We place a sprouting potato in a box with two baffles that will force the light-seeking growing tip to bend around corners. I will have to take it to a high shelf in the storeroom. Once the shutters of our classroom are closed, no light can enter, and besides, if the box were left there someone would destroy the whole thing. No room has any pictures or diagrams on the walls, no visual aids. I do not understand why they would quickly be torn down, any more than I can see why I can't leave a note on my front door for a friend who might come while I am out, or leave one on his door if I miss him. All I know is that it would infallibly be taken away. So, instead of leaving the growing plant to be watched all day by the succeeding classes, I will put it away and bring it out each day to show them its progress.

In their notebooks they make a drawing of the potato in its box. Then I bring out the leaves I had picked on the way to school and pass to every other child a parallel-veined bamboo leaf (monocot). The in-between children get an ageratum or hibiscus leaf with branching veins to show what a dicot is. "Draw your leaf as carefully as you can. Then change leaves with your neighbor and draw the other kind of leaf."

Soon, too soon, the children are holding up their drawings. "Miss, Miss, is mine right?" For child after child I hold a leaf up to the light and have him look more closely at the veins. "Look carefully at the shape of the leaf and the way the veins go, and draw it again."

When the bell rang I went to my next class and found Gobinda teaching it. Ram Bhakta had told me there were some changes in the schedule, but he hadn't told me I'd been relieved of the seventh grade class. No one had told me Gobinda had been given it to teach while I was away sick with a bout of hepatitis. I must have forced him to begin on time by innocently teaching the class yesterday before he appeared. Today he was there with unparalleled promptness and I realized what had happened.

I went back to the office and finished my diagrams of the flower and the bee to take to my next period, tenth grade biology, which I teach in the "library." It was locked, when I went to it, with a big iron lock. The new lock I had bought for it so this wouldn't happen is gone. (I had bought three keys to go with it and given two to Ram Bhakta.) Now the old lock with a single key was back on. I went to Ram Bhakta for the key. He didn't have it. The *piun* had taken it with him on an errand down to Banepa.

Four girls were waiting. "Will we have class today?" "Yes, we have a lot to learn today. We will sit on the grass."

One boy, Ratna Lall, appeared. He hesitated, but came up. Siddi Bahadur came up and said, "We can have the eighth grade room; the teacher isn't at school today so the room is empty." Ram Kaji came in and Bimala Devi. I showed my diagrams of the fertilization of the flower and the class exclaimed, "*Ramro chha.*" Yes it is beautiful, but do they understand what it means?

We had been studying the parts of a flower (this was a question that often appeared on the SLC exam) and they all knew, I thought, that pollen must get to the stigma of the flower or it could never produce fruit.

"Bimala Devi," I said. "Will you come up here and show on the diagram just how the bee is putting pollen on the stigma of the flower?" Bimala Devi stood, but could not bring herself to walk to the front of the room. Finally Siddi Bahadur came up and explained the whole process to the class. He, at least, had got it. But did Bimala Devi understand?

I gave them a short written quiz on it, another of my innovations. On the last quiz no one answered anything. They just copied the questions and stared at me. This time most of them answer. Even Bimala Devi gets 50%. I feel good.

That was the morning. There is no girls' latrine at school. I would not wander out to find a bush, the way the poor girls must do, in spite of my protests to Ram Bhakta about their plight. So I started down the mile long path to my *ghar* for lunch. Over my head I held a big black umbrella. This time of year you always need an umbrella, either for rain or the fierce sun that comes out right after it. I heard a call behind me. Siddi Bahadur was running to catch up with me. He has written a poem he wants to read to me. He reads it beautifully, his voice full and caressing on the sonorous double repetitions. Not a sing-song but a strongly accented beat. It is in Newari, so I have to ask what it is about. It is a love song about a girl, but Siddi Bahadur earnestly says, "It is only a poem." He has no girl in mind. He doesn't look at the girls in class. If he walks up the street with his arm around anybody it is another boy. But his poem is about a girl.

I hurried home for lunch and back up the hill for my afternoon classes. I knew that when I finished my last class I would come out of the room to a deserted school. All the other classes and teachers would already have gone home. The *piun* alone would be waiting to see me come out. He would then ring the bell and lock up, close the shutters, and go home. School would be over for another day. The next day it would begin at ten when I opened my first class. Once Asha Kaji told me he, too, would begin his classes on time, and for a while two classes began the school day promptly. But not for long.

Now the interesting part of this comedy was not that I was working my heart out trying, while the Nepali teachers sat and rested. We were all behaving as our culture dictated—I with my Western will to work, my insistence that whatever job was worth doing was worth doing to the best of my ability, my feeling of obligation to the few students who were trying to learn, and my (sometimes at least) interest and even joy in the work in spite of frustrations and difficulties.

The Nepalis, too, were acting out their roles. They were punctilious in signing the time book (which I was forever forgetting)—in at ten, out at four—no matter what time they really arrived or left. They maintained their *tulo manche* importance and disdain for hurry or energetic activity, and their sound feeling that the less you did the less chance you had of offending someone, or exposing yourself to the possibility of making mistakes. This has been the classic approach of job-holders all over the East from time immemorial.

And, to do them justice, they were so ill paid that many taught classes in morning school before ours began, and tutored at home in the evening to make ends meet. They were paid only $12 a month, and those who did not live with big and supportive families were hard put to it.

But the unhurried leisurely approach was not just due to poor pay. Almost any home or religious activity, and these occurred very very frequently, took precedence over school. And if you failed your SLC you took it again. Om Bahadur was my student as well as my cook. When he failed the all-important test I said, "But Om Bahadur, you didn't try. You hardly ever came to class. What will you do now?"

"I'll go to school next year and take it again."

"If my sons had not worked hard," I said severely, "We would not have paid to send them back to school."

"My father will pay."

"How long will he keep on paying if you fail again?" I asked, being quite sure that Om Bahadur would *never* be able to pass.

With the engaging smile that stretched his mouth and nearly closed his Oriental eyes, Om Bahadur replied, "*Sandai.*" (Forever.)

8

A Secret Westerners Have

IN MAY the school held the first of three exams—something new; before this there had been only one final test. As I walked up to school that day, the town seemed full of newborn pigs. All the sows were swollen with milk or babies. Their black bristles parted under the rain. They ran squealing out of the way, expecting always to be stoned. They knew they were untouchables.

Monsoon was starting early, and the streets were mud between irregular stones. The place where the path went between banks was a small river. Nothing for it but to wade. At one point I lost a thong sandal to the sucking mud and had to pull it out by hand. Then the rain stopped and the terraced fields and piled clouds were suddenly extraordinarily beautiful in the clean air.

At school the students were being seated so that no two taking the same examination sat side by side. My seventh grade tests were due to be given in two minutes, but they were still being mimeographed on the new machine the school was so proud of. They weren't coming out right. The paper was sticking together; only one in seven was being printed.

A stranger came hurrying in. When he put mimeograph paper in the machine instead of the thin cheap paper the Headmaster was trying to use, the exam papers started coming through. I had written multiple-choice, short-answer exams of the kind we had practiced in class. And Ram Bhakta had gone over my Nepali, but there were a number of mistakes and misprints. I went to all the classrooms where my seventh grade children were scattered and wrote corrections on the wooden blackboards.

46

I came to the classroom where Kedar Nath was invigilating. (They use the English word for this foreign activity.) A few children were writing busily; the rest were looking at the papers of those behind or in front of them, those of the pupils taking the same test they were. Whispered questions and answers flew softly back and forth. I looked at Kedar Nath. "Eh, eh," he grunted at the room and for a minute every eye returned to its proper sphere of interest.

I went into another room where another set of children and two more teachers were acting out the same comedy. The teachers wandered up and down the aisles, in and out of the classrooms, studiedly looking over the heads of the test takers. When Ram Bhakta came into a room the deference to the Headmaster stopped the cheating, but his presence was the only one that gave it pause.

As the exam progressed, hands began going up with requests to leave the room. In Nepali it is bluntly put. "I must go and urinate." When the boy or girl came back he would tell all his friends the answer he had looked up. It is a sharing community, and they were generous with their knowledge, if it can be called that.

Still the invigilating teachers noticed nothing. After all, the children had paid to take the tests (though only a few *paisa*); hadn't they a right to pass? It was their school and their system. It was obviously much too well accepted for me to do anything about it. I just resolved never to invigilate.

From then on I didn't go to school during the ten days of exams except when my own tests were scheduled, and then I only checked to see that they were printed correctly. But my detachment was not to last. One day Gobinda said to me with his elfin smile, "You don't like to invigilate, Root?"

I muttered something noncommital, but next day I was handed a slip of paper with a room assignment for the following day. Each class was scattered through several rooms and there were supposed to be two invigilating teachers assigned to every room, but their practice was to wander in and out of all the rooms. I knew they had ganged up on me when no one came near my room during the whole two hours.

Since I was there and supposedly in charge, I couldn't ignore the cheating, but I found myself completely unable to stop it. I was up against a whole social system. I didn't feel it would be fair (what a farce of conflicting cultures and motives) to tear up papers of, for instance, my five cheating math exam takers, when I knew their classmates were cheating with impunity in the other rooms. I wrote a note on the papers of those whom I caught *in flagrante delicto*, but they indignantly crossed out my remarks. The teacher who corrected the exams wouldn't care anyway, so mine was a futile gesture.

By the time the exam was ending and there were only two laboring students left I was exhausted with impotent outrage. How could any school call this a test? Then I saw that one of the boys had a pony in his lap. I held out my hand. "*Malai dinous na* (give it to me)," I said. He looked at me a second, put the paper in his mouth and began to swallow.

At that moment Issor Bhakta, the math teacher who had been assigned to invigilate with me, strolled in. "Issor Bhakta," I yelled. "Shubhadra was cheating and when I asked for the paper he was copying from he swallowed it." "Tsch, tsch," said Issor Bhakta.

I was still trembling with indignation and frustration as I collected the tests and went to talk to the Headmaster. Ram Bhakta listened and then said, "You don't have to invigilate any more exams." Perhaps he really wanted to stop the cheating, but it was too much for him, too. I suggested that they not allow the children to go out to the latrine. "They only look up the answers and come back and tell everyone."

At the next teachers' meeting it was decided to make the exams shorter and not allow anyone to leave. That lasted through the following exam. Then back to the good old system.

Cheating doesn't mean that brains don't win out; intelligence is just applied in a different way. In 1969-70 the best student in my tenth grade cass preparing for the SLC test was Siddi Bahadur, my young poet. He would come to class primed with questions he wanted clarified. At home he went over and over all the old SLC exams he could get hold of. Then he would get me to review the biology answers in class. However, he would have thought it foolhardy to trust even his good memory for this vital test.

Om Bahadur was taking the test also. After he knew he had failed, he told me, "I thought we would have to name the 10 kinds of modified roots, and the differences between plant and animal cells, and draw the external aspect of the rabbit." (Om Bahadur had seen the old tests too). "But Siddi Bahadur thought we would get all the questions we did get." Poor Om Bahadur had taken the wrong cribs to the exam. Well, better luck next year.

The questions for the SLC exam were state secrets guarded by the army. It was always possible that a teacher who knew the questions might betray them to a favored pupil, just as some deliberately taught sketchily in class, or even in textbooks, so that they could give the "real" facts to pupils who paid to be tutored after school. So the army kept the tests until exam day.

More destructive still was the prevalent belief that the SLC or a college degree is the end of learning and work, the passport to importance and a cushy position. Education is something that gets you somewhere, not a tool to be used. Nepalis were learning facts; the principles and concepts that explain the facts they had no use for.

For my seventh grade unit on mechanics I was trying one day to put into Nepali the concept of friction for our study of how tools work. After trying to help me translate my definition into Nepali, Ram Bhakta asked in polite but puzzled tones, "Do they need to know that?" A smooth ball rolls faster than a rough one. Never mind why. Friction, gravity, inertia, deductive reasoning? Of what use are they?

We Westerners are a constant enigma. There must be some secret we possess, some magic key that enables us to carry around all sorts of luxurious clothes and gadgets. There is a glimmering idea that the secret is locked somewhere in this mass of information to be learned in school. One day, the Nepalis were sure, they would stumble upon it. In the meantime, if they asked for my flashlight or my sweater, perhaps I would give it to them.

Were my classes, as I struggled to make them think, studying me to see what it was about me that gave me my watch, and camera, and tape recorder? My down jacket?

The secrets I was trying to impart to them were hard work and advance planning. But my kind of work and planning were too strange to them. Their world worked otherwise.

Take for instance, the wonderful festivals, or take especially the Festival of Chandeshwari, which was an occasion of pilgrimage for towns and villages many miles away. Its day was fixed by the moon and the heavens and was printed in the sacred calendar. People would gather early in the morning. The priests and leaders who were to ride on the god's chariot, the *rath*, from Banepa to Chandeshwari's Temple across the valley, all knew their duties. The men who would carry the heavy *rath* knew theirs, each fixed by his caste and position. The spectators waited patiently around the *rath* with its red and white streamers, its gold, and flowers. Eventually the procession would start. When the spirit moved them the priests would climb to their positions on the *rath*; men would shoulder the great beams; little boys would run ahead. Ponderously the *rath* would move a few feet while the audience stirred with excitement to see the bedecked god in his gloriously decorated conveyance. The great religious festival had begun to unfold.

When the spirit is ready they move. There is no hurry. No

one minds waiting. Time is not money, and if it were, money is not the essence. It is pleasant to sit with your friends and wait for the gods to arrive and the worship to begin.

Life, the day, and the year all have an underlying pattern known to everyone. Though they are prescribed in detail, they seem improvised at the last moment. When I was invited to eat a *bhoj* at someone's house a messenger would hammer on my door and bid me come. Come right now. When things were planned ahead, such as a picnic, or a trip to a distant shrine to see its famous statue, they usually didn't happen.

In school it was that way too. At the end of the first year Ram Bhakta asked me to write the book to be used the next year.

"Oh, Ram Bhakta, that's a terribly big job. Of course every teacher would like to write his own text, but . . ."

"The books are no good. You don't use them much. If you will write it in English, I will translate it to Nepali and we'll have it mimeographed."

"That's an awfully big job." Then, "I have my outlines and lesson plans. Maybe I could write a study guide, but you would have to give me a light teaching schedule. Which class do you want me to write it for?"

"I will make out the school schedule and inform you."

"All right. I'll come back early from my vacation. I'll take a very short one and come back so I can get the first month's work written and you can translate and mimeograph it before school starts."

So I tore myself away from the fascinations of Agra, and Khajuraho, and Mahabalipuram, and rushed back—to wait. Which grade was I to plan for? Which text was I to write? Long ago I had made a graduated and progressing curriculum. No longer would even one lesson be the same for all.

I waited until all but two days of vacation were gone before Ram Bhakta made up his mind that he wanted the text for the sixth grade. Time to plan and work? *Now* the book is needed. Start writing it.

Somehow I did it, and it proved to be a big help, but I am sure that the flimsy pages it was mimeographed on didn't survive long after that year. As far as I know no other teacher ever used it. Even so, it was something accomplished and anything I could consider an accomplishment was rare. Problems that could not be solved and contretemps were the usual order of things.

Why didn't I give up? Of the group of 72 that had started Peace Corps training as *Nepal 18*, most did give up; 46 actually went to Nepal, and 19 stayed the allotted 2 years. Three of us stayed longer. I was tempted to quit, but I had come to love Nepal—for its beauty, the warmth of its people, and for the exciting, colorful religious worship and festivals which were part and parcel of it.

There was, for instance, the prospect always dancing before me of the Dasain fortnight of festival just as Monsoon ceased. Freed from school I would go trekking up toward the snow mirages hovering on the northern horizon, joining in some of the village festivals as I went.

And the school itself held me. Infuriating as it was in so many ways, it was a challenging problem. Looked at as a challenge, even the most outrageous aberrations assumed the aspect of bits of input to be figured in. After all, the whole school system, and the Ministry of Education, were only a few years old. They were wonderful if one considered they had risen from nothing.

There were also the children. No matter how poor they were as students some of them were delightful friends that I will never forget. And how could I give up when in every class there were one or two pupils who were really trying to learn. In the end I taught for them. They deserved the best I could give. Janak and Yegya were two of these. Janak's smile of comprehension when he got the point I was driving at was the stuff a teacher would trade his right arm for. Taro, Dipak, and Praneswari fixed me with their serious attention always. Siddi Bahadur had

learned to work by himself and use my knowledge to enlarge
the picture of Biology he was building in his mind.

One day Janak and Yegya said to me, "When you teach us we
understand."

Conscious always of my failings, I said, "Oh, but I still wish
my Nepali were so much better."

"But when you teach us we *understand*. In the other classes
we just memorize what the book says. You explain things so
they make sense."

That day I walked on clouds.

9

Rice On A Gold Coin

GUNGA LALL'S HOUSE had a shop front on the bazaar and a back window that looked out into our court. At this window, day after day, sat a little girl. It is hard for a Westerner to tell the age of the tiny, neatly made Nepalis. I believe that Om Devi was fourteen years old, though at first I thought her about eight.

One day as I sat on the *bichona* in front of my window preparing a science lesson, I saw her on the roof. She and her brother, Hari Lall, who was one of my students, were spreading rice to dry. They poured the golden stream of just-harvested rice out of round baskets and spread it with wooden rakes. Om Devi trod the rice with bare feet. Her bright blue sari swayed as she worked.

She looked up and smiled at her brother as she raked and stirred and spread the rice. Stepping backward she approached closer and closer to the edge of the roof. Suddenly Hari Lall yelled, ran over and grabbed her, and pulled her back. She looked at him and laughed merrily.

I hadn't understood his words; I wondered idly what she was laughing at. He pushed her down to a sitting position and gave her a basket of red peppers and some string-like material. She deftly began to tie the peppers into a garland. Except for a few times on the roof, I saw Om Devi only at her window, from which now dangled several ropes of red peppers. She never went out into the court to play with the other children.

In that court all the business and ritual of life went on. Om Devi looked down on a rich tapestry whose pattern had endured for thousands of years. For each time and season there was a

Three of my neighbors winnowing grain with flat trays.

familiar ceremony. From planting to harvest, from birth to
death. Each person had his place—fixed on the loom when the
warp was set.

Interpreter of the ritual was the Newar priest who lived in a
room of the large house attached to mine. His sacred thread
hung across his bare chest. When he went to the neighborhood
faucet, he washed more thoroughly and longer than anyone else.
Often he sat in the sun reading his mantras. Next in our small
hierarchy came Krishna Maya and her family. Krishna Maya,
married at nine, mother of five, managed the affairs of the court
with a strident voice and a gentle hand. She called out advice, to
Om Devi at her window, to the tailor squatting on his mat as he
ran his hand-sewing machine, to Gian Bhakta, the goat man,
and to Om Devi's mother, who was about to bear another
child—or so it seemed by the heavily wrapped draperies over
her sari.

As Gian Bhakta brought his two sleek little black goats out of the ground-floor of his house, Krishna Maya called, "By the Ganesh temple at Wokutol there's a bunch of grass for your goats. I saw it when I took my offerings this morning. Go, take your *kukri* and cut it before someone else does."

Thin little Gian Bhakta gave her a shy smile and a *salam* with his hand to his forehead, tethered his goats by the wall, and went off after the grass. When he came back he called to her, "That was good grass, and I found some more along the bank of the rice paddy." He squatted to watch the goats eat. Their gold eyes stared contentedly back at him, as their lower lips moved rhythmically sidewise. He sat very close to watch because one of his eyes was opaque and the other already half clouded. When he heard Om Devi give a little laugh as one goat butted the other, he threw a quick smile toward her window.

Both he and the goats looked up expectantly whenever I walked their way, since I had started taking them the scraps and peelings from my kitchen. This was one of the intervals when I had no cook. I'd had to fire Om Bahadur for stealing.

Once I threw the goats some tiny wrinkled potatoes, but before they could begin to nibble, the matmaker's wife rushed out and snatched them away for her own dinner. The matmaker's family were the lowest caste people on our court. They were of the caste of sweepers, very low indeed. They offered to keep my doorstep swept for me, and to persuade me that it was necessary they swept their own debris onto it.

Each one, from high to low, spoke his mind in the court. Krishna Maya, the priest, the tailor, the matmaker, each had his say. Only Om Devi never offered an opinion. She merely smiled from her window. She was too young, I thought, and too shy to speak.

After morning worship of the gods at each family shrine and the carrying of offerings to all the nearby temples, came the morning meal. Its essential ingredient was *bhat*, cooked rice.

Bhat was the life-sustaining food, the principal and vital part of the two daily meals. It was sacred and could be eaten only with one's own family and caste. It could not even be accepted from the hand of a lower-caste person without pollution which then must be washed away by arduous rituals. After ten o'clock the universal greeting in the village was, *"Bhat khayo?"* (Have you eaten rice?)

At this time each day Om Devi stationed herself at her window in the court. Krishna Maya spread millet on a mat to dry. She sat for hours waving a bamboo pole over it when chickens or pigs stole too near.

A procession of quick-moving barefooted men went by, beating drums and blowing conch shells. On the way back from worshipping at Chandeshwari, they had detoured through our court to place offerings before the stone Buddha who sat on a stone lotus just around the corner.

The tailor worked on a shirt for one of the goldsmith's sons, keeping it carefully out of the dust around the mat where he sat crosslegged. Three tiny girls were playing a game with pebbles. One tumbled over, and Om Devi in her window laughed silently.

My second floor landing was directly across from her post. Whenever I passed by she would give me a beautiful smile and gesture *namaste* with her two joined hands respectfully at her forehead. I responded, as was proper, with mine at my breast.

One day she appeared with the tiny new baby, a pale-skinned little boy. When Om Devi saw me, her smile flashed and she lifted the infant for me to see. She moved the bits of hands into a *namaste* and I returned the gesture. Delight was on Om Devi's face as she hugged the baby tight.

One day Taro, a neighbor and one of my students, was visiting in my second-floor sitting room where I kept books and games. He stopped with a puzzle piece in his hand, his head raised to listen. From the bazaar we heard the approaching beat

of drums, horns, and cymbals. *"Aunos!"* (Come on!) said Taro
getting up from the floor. In the hall we slipped into our shoes,
ran down the stairs, and out the narrow alley to the bazaar.

Bhimsen, god of wealth, was coming down the bazaar in his
sedan chair carried by four men. He was made of gilded metal
and was decked with marigolds and dahlias. Musicians led the
way and the rest of us followed the god. Out of town we went,
across the river and, on raised paths, between rice paddies to the
small temple on the opposite slope. Taro took me inside the
walled enclosure where the god had come to rest in front of his
shrine. Women were bringing trays neatly arranged with
offerings of rice and flowers and red powder. Some held
squawking chickens by the feet. The god was already splatterd
with blood. Having nothing else, I offered a coin to the priest.
He touched it to his forehead and tossed it into the god's lap.

Toward the end of the afternoon, Bhimsen rode back to
Banepa on his devotees' shoulders to be installed in front of the
Shiva temple across from Gunga Lall's shop. Bhimsen is a
favorite of merchants. A crowd filled the bazaar. Krishna Maya
kept asking me to go get my *durupin* (binoculars). She wanted
me to take pictures. Binoculars or camera were all the same to
her, but it was already too dark.

Flaring lights began to reflect from the polished brass trays
full of offerings that a steady file of women were bringing to the
god. Their shadows jumped up and down as they threaded their
way forward. When a chicken was handed to the priest, he
wrung its neck and held it so the blood spurted into Bhimsen's
brass mouth. Some fell into a big brass pot. Some splattered on
the ground where the pi dogs fought to lick it up.

Torches flared brighter. Banners of incense floated on the air,
wafting strands of scent. People watched from windows and
house tops. They lined the high stone curbing which runs along
in front of the stores and forms that platform on which they are
built. Everyone was there; the faces of all my neighbors shone
out of the crowd.

Even Om Devi was out that night with the baby tied on her back. It was the first time I had been close to either of them. Om Devi twisted round to bring the baby nearer to me. Its big eyes opened wide, became alarmed. I was too strange at such close quarters. My white skin was frightening. I moved away quickly.

The priest, he who sat in the sun most days mildly reading his mantras, now loomed forbidding and unknown beside the god. He took up the halter of a little black goat and led it to the golden Bhimsen. Behind him I could see the diffident smile of Gian Bhakta. The sacrifice was the larger of the two goats he had tended so lovingly. The one he had asked me to photograph in his arms a few days ago.

Everyone pushed me forward so I could see. Hari Lall swept crowding children out of my view. I held back as far as I could. The goat stood quietly. Its little horns looked to me like a Greek faun's. Over the small black head the priest poured water and sprinkled *bhat*. He poured again and the sleek creature shook his head, giving consent to the sacrifice.

The priest put a marigold, some dahlia petals, and mulberry leaves between the horns. He cupped his hand with food under the goat's mouth, which automatically began to chew. He lifted the animal up in front of the god and quickly slit its throat. Most of the blood gushed into the bronze bowl. In a minute the priest handed the carcass back to Gian Bhakta.

He gazed into my shrinking face and said, *"Khana ko lagi."* (It is food.) "We'll have a feast and meat to eat. And maybe Bhimsen will bring us some money."

"I don't know about that," said Gunga Lall, who had been leaning over to listen, his finely modeled face serious. "In olden days there was a man who sacrificed to Bhimsen and prayed to him. When he woke the next morning there was a pile of gold beside his pallet. I never hear of anything like that nowadays."

"Well, anyway, he'll keep me from bad luck, I hope. And, for tomorrow, there is a feast." Gian Bhakta patted the still-sleek flank of the goat.

Om Devi slid to the back of the shop past bolts of cloth. As she went by, her father took the baby from her back and held it up toward the golden Bhimsen glittering in the torch flare.

"See, Littlest One," he said, dandling it, "That's the god who brings riches. When you are a man, he will bring us lots of gold, and you, Hari Lall, and I will be partners."

In front of him a group of boys crowded close to the ceremonies. The girls stood separately, pressed back against the wall. Om Devi was not with them. She came from the back of the shop with four red dahlias to hand to her mother. The mother was squatting before a shining brass tray arranging a pile of cooked rice, pieces of cucumber and guava, red powder. She put the dahlias in the center, gave the tray a satisfied look, and stood up adjusting her sari. Om Devi stooped for the tray and lifted it to her mother, who took it over to the priest.

"Look, Littlest, my wife is making offerings to the god," said Gunga Lall. "Good fortune will come." He handed the baby back to Om Devi. She stationed herself behind the other girls, her eyes shining in the firelight.

I told the children at school that I needed a live bird for my biology class. The next day Hari Lall came to my door with a sparrow in his hands.

"How did you catch it?" I asked, opening the door of a bamboo cage.

"I scattered a little *bhat* on the floor after we finished eating, and several sparrows flew in. I grabbed one. The baby wanted to keep it. He cried."

"What is the baby's name?"

"He doesn't have a name yet. He'll get one when he first eats *bhat*. We Newars have a special ceremony when a baby first eats cooked rice. We will take him to the temple, and we'll have a feast. And all the relatives will come, even from Sanku and Budol. We will feed the baby with a gold coin. It is the same one I first ate *bhat* from. So did my father and grandfather."

"How old must he be before he eats *bhat*?"

"Eight months. For a boy it must be eight months or six months."

Just then a scream shrilled from Krishna Maya's window. I jumped. Several neighbors were running to the house, Om Devi's mother among them. Hesitantly, I went over too. "What is the matter?" I asked. Om Devi's mother said, "Krishna Maya's younger sister died yesterday. They cremated her last night. Krishna Maya was there, of course. She can't stop thinking of her sister."

"Oh, how terrible! What did she die of?"

"She just got sick and died."

"Did the Doctor come?"

"Yes, the Nepali Doctor, the Shaman. It was too late. He could not save her."

Krishna Maya was swaying back and forth in a huddle on the floor, moaning. Half an hour later she was staring sadly out of her window, but by evening she was calling jokes to the neighbors as usual, though her face was drawn.

The baby in Om Devi's arms was growing day by day. He seemed to see me now; his smiles focused on my face clear across the court. One day when Hari Lall came to visit, I asked him why Om Devi seldom went out.

"*Lati ho.*" (She is dumb.)

Then I realized that with all her smiles and gestured *namastes* I had never heard her speak. I redoubled my smiles and so did she. And, at her direction, so did the baby, whose hair now curled softly around his face. His eyes were enormous, with a smear of black collyrium, a beautification and protection against evil that all babies wear. He had taken to making *namaste* with his own tiny hands whenever he saw me at my window.

There was a holiday, and I went to Kathmandu for a few days. The morning after my return I started for school. A small crowd stood at the alley door of Om Devi's house. Inside, on the ground at the foot of the stairs, lay the pale baby in the place where a dying person must be laid. His minute tunic, the only garment he wore, was turned back above his navel. His mouth was open and a trickle of blood ran out of one corner. Three old men squatted around him. One was pouring holy water into his mouth. In a dark corner at the back of the room, a bundle of cloth was choking and gasping. It was Om Devi. Her mother and grandmother were quietly weeping. The group outside the door was immobile and quiet.

"What happened?" I whispered to Krishna Maya.

"He is dying."

"But why? What happened?"

"He just got sick."

Was it cholera, of which there was some in town? Or some less dread malady? I was never to know. But as I stood listening to the weeping of Om Devi I suddenly realized who the real mother of the baby was. How? Who? No matter. Somehow in that silent guarded life she had found someone of her own. The language of loving touch had needed no voice. And now—she was bereft.

The old men felt the baby's swollen belly, straightened his legs, upended the bronze vessel, and poured more water into the little mouth and over the navel. They felt his arms. I could barely see a small rise and fall of the chest against the back-turned tunic. They poured more water from the jar (it had been quickly refilled) on his curly baby hair. They waited. Gunga Lall, his fine face quiet, sat at the baby's feet.

Again the old men touched the baby gently, straightened again the paling limbs, poured water on the genitals. They were officials of Gunga Lall's *guthi* or funeral association. Impassively they awaited the moment of death. In all that group of old and young, my eyes were the only ones that had never looked on a dying.

From the open door Hari Lall handed in some incense-filled wicks. Krishna Maya made a gesture to her youngest son, Rajhan. He went away and was back in a minute with a small brown bottle full of oil. The old men were pouring more holy water on the face and in circles over and around the body. They placed small clay dishes at the baby's head and feet, filled them with oil from the brown bottle and lit the wicks. Everyone in the house went upstairs. I walked on to school.

I taught my classes and came back two and a half hours later. In Gunga Lall's house there was nothing on the ground between the foot of the stairs and the door but two small, burned out and blackened clay dishes. The tiny body had already been confided to the river, a sacred river, as all flowing water is holy in Nepal. The child was too young to be cremated. He had never yet eaten *bhat*. He had no name.

From the house came the sound of low wailing. A couple of dozen men filed in, members of the funeral association, and a few women with trays under their shawls. Little Om Devi was leaning stoically against the window frame. Slowly, she turned back into the house.

Next morning, in the sunniest part of the court there were pans and bowls of water. All the women of the dead baby's family had their hair flowing unbraided and were wailing loudly. They washed their hair, and all the clothes of the family. They scoured all the pots and vessels. Everything in the house must be cleaned of death pollution. All this time the court was full as usual. One man was shaving; Rajhan was fixing a wheel on a toy wooden cart; the matmaker's wife waved a pole over rice brought out again to dry.

The baby is gone, but in six months there will come *gai jatra,* the festival of the cow. That is the time when spirits can find rest. In every house where someone died during the year there is a ceremony. Afterward, a young male relative comes out dressed to represent a cow.

Hari Lall, if he doesn't look like a cow, at least has a tall conical basket over his head with a painted cow's face attached to it—a paper cow's face bought in the bazaar for five *paisa*. The basket is covered with streamers of cloth and an old shirt whose two arms stick out in a semblance of horns. Behind him walks another child holding a black umbrella over Hari Lall's head. In Kathmandu, rich children parade in brocade and flowers while an attendant carries a red and orange fringed umbrella of the kind used for gods. In Banepa, an old black umbrella has to do.

The streets are full of cow children going from shrine to shrine. Some cows are being led on the rounds too. One of them has a paper cow's face attached to her own bovine forehead. People offer cakes, sweetmeats, and rice to the children. They put garlands around the necks of the cows. Om Devi leans out of her window to watch it all, but I see a tear in her eye.

When Hari Lall comes home, I beckon him to me. "It was for the baby that I went to the temples today," he tells me. "Do you know about Yama's house? It is where people who die want to go. Today is the only day of the year when the gates are not fastened tight and our mother the cow can open them with her horns. So we dress like cows, and worship cows, and go to the temples of the gods. And now our baby will go to Yama's house and be safe."

His smile is confident and serene. I look at the window. Om Devi's smile echoes his, though her cheek is still wet. The threads of life and death, of love and loss, run near together. In the close-knit fabric a stitch that had been dropped is now secured. The fabric is whole.

10

An Ogre Dies in Banepa

I WAS CONSTANTLY BEING SURPRISED by something new in Banepa. One day it was a little man about three feet tall sitting in front of the Dakshin Kali temple in the bazaar. For two days and nights he sat there under a black umbrella. His black moustaches curled fiercely. He wore black clothing, heavy gold earrings, and an old-fashioned turban whose like had not been seen in Nepal for 200 years.

At first, all I could learn was what I could see. He was made of cooked rice. My questions were answered, *"Bhatko manche ho."* He is the man of cooked rice. When they started to tell me his story, it was my fellow teacher Krishna Prasad who told it best. Krishna Prasad himself wears black clothing. He has enormous mournful eyes. His smile shows badly neglected teeth, if one can speak of neglect where care is unknown. But he told his story as a poet would. The *bhatko manche* is the effigy of an ogre who used to live in our valley. He caught and devoured people, and everyone was terrified by his very shadow.

In those days Banepa had a courageous Headman who managed to meet and treat with the ogre. He persuaded the ogre to let the villagers cook him a big meal of rice and curry every day and to be satisfied with that instead of eating people. But the ogre would not forego his favorite meal entirely. The Headman had to promise that once a year they would send him a man, or a woman, or a full-grown child to eat.

One year the lot fell to a Jyapu of the farmer caste named Jiban. It happened that a traveller had stopped at Jiban's *ghar* that afternoon. Jiban's wife fed him, and Jiban offered him a pallet to sleep on. Not till the guest was sleeping could Jiban speak freely to his family. "Dear wife and son," he said. "I will bid you farewell now, for before tomorrow's light I must go to the ogre. Take care of each other when I am gone. Son, perform the death rites faithfully and carefully, so that my spirit may rest and watch over you both."

But the wife, though she trembled as she spoke, said, "No, I will go. You are my lord. I cannot let you go to your death."

And the son cried, "No, I will go. You are my parents. I kiss your feet. It is my duty to go instead of you."

Except for the oriental details, the story began to sound familiar. Here, half a world away, was a tale of Grimm or Andersen. Only this wasn't safely encased in a book. Here sat the ogre fiercely staring at me.

I wasn't surprised when Krishna Prasad went on, "The guest had overheard them. He was the King's son in disguise." (Of course! I thought.) "He jumped up and claimed the right to meet the ogre. Jiban tried to dissuade him and they all wailed to see him go. But when he met the ogre, he drew his jeweled *kukri* and killed the evil being with one mighty blow."

Krishna Prasad tilted his head quickly sideways, greeting a friend who was passing, and finished his story. "The noble prince set the valley free from terror. All the people rejoiced, and every year since then, we celebrate the deliverance of Banepa with the *bhatko manche*."

So the ogre sat in the bazaar under his umbrella till on the third day the people lifted him into the red-canopied sedan chair. Musicians led the way and we all followed. My student, Tika Bhakta, took me along in the midst of the crowd.

"Where are we going, Tika Bhakta?" I asked, and he answered, "To the river."

Everyone trooped along in festive mood while drums banged and conch shells blasted. Swallows sailed past our ankles in the street. The sun shone brightly. We reached the river close to the burning ghat. Tika found me a place to stand. A big man lifted the ogre in his arms and carried him down the bank to the river's edge. Drawing his *kukri*, he slashed at the ogre's stomach. He used the same weapon to kill the ogre that the prince in the story did. It was the same vicious knife with which the famed Gurkha soldiers fight even today. He slashed, and a great flow of blood gushed out.

"What is that?" I gasped. "Pig's blood," said Tika Bhakta under his breath. "He doesn't have the same circulatory system we have been studying in class."

He grinned at me and stooped to pick up a stone. Suddenly the air was full of rocks. The people of Banepa were screaming at the ancient enemy and stoning him to death. They kept on hurling stone after stone at his battered body, ecstatic with his death.

I remembered a little village near Nice in France. There they hold a religious procession every year to commemorate the time in 1468 when their Roquebrune Village survived the plague, while all around it people were dying. Corpses began to be piled in the streets of Roquebrune, too. All hope seemed gone. But the blessed Virgin heard their prayers. The worst of the dread disease passed them by, and Roquebrune's population mostly lived. I thought again how like medieval European life the life here was. Its constant celebrations, almost all of them religious. Its apportionment of a large part of every day to worship. The closeness between people and deities. The color and significance that filled the days, beginning with the obligatory daily ceremonies of worship. Matins, to the catholics of Europe.

The prince and the ogre weren't religious figures, but feudal. Their story could have happened anywhere in medieval Europe. So could what happened the next day.

When I went up to school the whole faculty was there. Ram Bhakta explained that we were going to a hill 4 miles to the east to inaugurate a new holy place, a *Mahadev pokhari*. A few weeks earlier, a man of the town of Dhulikhel had had a vivid dream or vision. Shiva, the great god, Mahadev, had appeared to him and commanded him to make a pool on that hill. It should be sacred to Shiva. There would be a great *mela*, or fair, by the new pool today, and we must all go. So, happily abandoning classes, the whole school started off. A large crowd of Nepalis were walking in the same direction. As usual I was the only Westerner. A trail led along the dikes between rice paddies, and over some steep fields, a path new to me. I almost tripped over a cut end of barbed wire. Looking around I could see that a big area here had been fenced. A few seedling trees, only inches high, persisted from a planting the government had hopefully made. The rest had been eaten by cattle and water buffaloes, let in through numerous cuts in the wire. The few survivors of this projected forest would soon go, giving the monsoon rains free rein to wash the soil away. I could see the erosion well begun already.

As we got closer to the hill of our destination I saw two square pools dug in the field. They were very muddy. Across one, three long bamboo poles had been laid, and above the center there was a square of orange cloth with a red ruffle. It represented a temple to be built sometime in the future when some wealthy man desired to acquire merit. Below it, supported by the bamboo poles, but half in the water, was a sort of bag serving as an altar. Squatting in front of this, balancing on the bending bamboos, was a priest in black *topi* and a vest worn over a more or less white *dhoti-suruwal*. We all handed our offerings to Gobinda, who reached them out to the priest and returned with red powder on his third finger-tip to give us each a *tika* on the forehead.

Jnan Kaji took me over to the other pool where men in breechclouts and barebreasted women were bathing in the thick water. Jnan Kaji watched them and smiled at me. His smile called me to admire and appreciate the religious beauty he saw. It was one of the times when, though I tried to see through Nepali eyes, I could not quite do it. I was too effete. I wanted the water clean and clear. What I did see was that the whole celebration was uplifting and inspiring to everyone else there.

Their eyes shone. They had the beginning of a new holy place, the beneficent presence of the Great God, and a fair with merchants selling food, drink, and a few gaudy souvenirs. And it was another confirmation of solidarity among themselves, another tie linking past and present, and future, god and human. But there was no solemnity about it. They were having such fun; it was easy to be happy with them.

New holy place for Shiva Mahadev is inaugurated while the new-dug pool is still muddy and the temple is indicated by a red and orange canopy. A Hindu priest accepts offerings and gives the devotees *prasad*—a part of their own offerings blessed by the god.

However, my problems at school continued. One thing that constantly plagued me was that hardly anyone else came to class on time. Of course they did not have clocks at home, so I would try allowing five minutes before I started getting into the meat of the lesson. No matter how long I waited, some were sure to come late and stand on the sill, crying "May I come, Sir?"

I tried to get the *piun* to stand outside my door and refuse entry to those who were tardy. I would be laboring to help them build a logical train of thought, when, "May I come, Sir?" would resound from the doorway and every eye would turn toward the new pupil, every mind would go back to blank.

Eventually I realized that the *piun* wouldn't keep them out. Everyone was sure they had a right to come in, even if their entry destroyed all vestiges of thought in the class. I tried to get them to slip in quietly. That didn't help. I begged them to be on time. No good. Promptness did not fit their way of life, but then, of course, neither did analytic reasoning.

Still, I had my heart in teaching them, and I had to keep on trying. It was a wearing business. Toward the beginning of my second summer, I became so exhausted that it frightened me. I was trembling tired and afraid that I would somehow break. If I did, I wanted someone to know that I was aware of what was happening to me. I went up to the Adventist Hospital across the valley to see my friend, Dr. Clark, to tell him of my exhaustion.

Luckily a two-week break was due and I set off like a somnambulist for Kashmir. Somehow I got the flight to Delhi, changed planes, and arrived in Srinigar. I'd been advised, by another volunteer, to stay on Nageen Lake instead of the much more crowded Dall Lake. In the airport I found the owner of a houseboat on Nageen. Or rather, he found me. Gratefully I put myself in his hands.

He took me to a floating small hotel, all my own. Moored

next to it was another boat where all my servants lived. They cooked me delicious meals. They pampered me. They let me rest. When I wished to go anywhere, I had my own *shikarra*, a canopied boat which would noiselessly arrive at the foot of the steps from my veranda to waft me around the lake. Most of the time I reclined in a deck chair and rested, looking languidly at the beautiful lake and the snowy mountains. A tiny jeweled Eurasian kingfisher would sit on a wire beside me on the top of the houseboat. Sometimes merchants would be paddled by in their little boats and would bring their wares onto my porch or into the living room that opened off it. Old silver, numdah rugs, wools embroidered all over in wonderful crewel designs, tankas from Tibet, carvings of strange woods. Kashmiris are the most persistent salesmen in the world. Several times, I woke to find a boat outside my window, the merchant standing with eyes fixed on my face, waiting for the first flutter of consciousness.

Now and then, I would summon my *shikarra* and lie back against the cushions to be paddled gently on the quiet waters with a heart-shaped paddle wielded by a boatman standing erect at the stern of the boat. I watched the reflections of the trees and the mountains, looked at the strange birds, one especially who walked on the lily pads. Once I summoned energy to visit the Shalimar Gardens with their flower beds and their huge old chinar trees, 12 feet in diameter.

After a week I felt sufficiently recovered to be driven up to the high meadows of Gulmarg, and to ride a pony on up through the evergreen forest paved with rosy and blue primroses. We, my landlord-cicerone and I, headed for the snow. It was a marvel to the Indians from the hot plains below. They had never been near this cold slippery stuff before. Local boys were pulling them a couple of hundred feet up the slope on sleds, then jumping on behind and guiding the sled on a breathless descent which made the plainsmen scream with excitement. It was a wonderful and exotic amusement.

I rested another day on the houseboat, enjoying every second of beauty and luxurious idleness. Then it was time to pack my bag and fly back to my *charpi*, my mud-floored kitchen, my one-burner kerosene stove. I must go back and start trying again. Trying again.

I sighed, thinking of medieval Europe once more. In the monasteries of the 15th century students may have been concerned with how many angels could teeter on the head of a pin, not with science, but at least they were in class on time.

11

The Little Girls and the Elephant-Headed God

I T WAS A STRANGE CONFRONTATION, that between the Western idol, science, and the ancient gods of Nepal. Inductive reasoning, logical explanation, and the clean cold fascination of an ordered world where things move in ways humans can understand and predict—what had any of that to do with a land where gods and demons live everywhere and control everything? A land where men and women devote endless time to propitiation and worship of the divine and holy forces that surround them?

I shouldn't call it a confrontation. The gods never knew I was teaching science. They accepted my offerings of rice or money as graciously as they did the spurting blood of animal sacrifice offered by others. My offerings at the school—offerings of thoughts, of ideas, of methods—floated softly over the heads of most of my students and disturbed the gods not at all.

The celestial host I had directly to deal with was my class— Shiva, Ganesh, Narayan, Indra, and the rest. Their feet were bare on the mud floor, but gold flashed from their ears, and they were named for gods that were old when the world was young.

On the front bench of my sixth grade class sat four little girls pressed snugly together. Four small goddeses—Renuka Devi, Indra Devi, Chetana Devi, and Jiban Devi, very beautiful with sculptured, tilted eyes, the clear whites accented by a black line drawn on the upper lid. When they thought I wasn't looking they would giggle and murmur softly to each other. Then for a few minutes all four would regard me with an unwavering gaze.

73

One day after school they surrounded me as I started down the path to Banepa. *"Banepa ramro chha? Ho ki Miss?"* "Yes," I said, "Banepa is very nice." This was often the opening gambit of my students' conversations. Renuka said, "We want you to come to dinner at my house."

"How kind of you. How shall I find your house?"

"We will come and get you."

In an hour they arrived at my door, two of them with babies tied on their backs with shawls. They led me into a part of town I had not visited before, through a warren of narrow alleys. We passed into a closed courtyard with the statue of a god in the center, through a dark ground floor where a cow munched peacefully on beanstalks, and up two flights of stairs. We left our shoes at the top of the first flight, of course. Barefoot, we went into a small room that faced the valley and the Mahabharat Lekh. The girls had a flat white cushion ready for me to sit on. Renuka with her baby brother and Chetana with her baby sister stayed with me while Jiban and Indra went upstairs. "We have everything ready," said Renuka holding her brother up on his wobbly legs and walking him over to sit beside her on the floor. The girls came back with fresh *chapattis*, rice, spicy vegetable curry, a fried egg, and small plum-like pickled fruits. "What a *bhoj*," I said, and we all began to eat with our right hands.

After food came entertainment. They urged the baby girl, Chetana's sister, to dance for us, and laughed gaily with her when she tumbled over. Renuka stood up with a serious face, raised her arms, and did a graceful dance while the others sang in soft voices. Then they took me into the next room to meet Renuka's mother and grandmother. We all sat on the floor and made pleasant inquiries of each other. "How many children do you have?" "Do you like Banepa?" "Is Renuka's husband selected?" The answer to that was, "Not yet. We must collect more money for her dowry first." "But here is my sister who is married and has three children and lives in Biratnagar in the

Terai," said Renuka showing me a snapshot. "Did she go to school? Will your little sister go to school?" They answered that Renuka was the first in the family to go. Her little sister would be educated too.

"Tomorrow is Tuesday," I said. On Tuesdays I always saw the trail going up beside our small river filled with people on their way to worship. "Are you going up to the Ganesh temple on the mountain?"

"Yes, every Tuesday we must go. Miss, come with us. Come with us."

"What must I bring for offerings?" I asked.

"Nothing. We will bring everything."

At 4:15 next morning Ganesh Lall's bell woke me. Ganesh Lall was the owner of the house behind mine, the high house with a large walled courtyard and a cow in the ground floor room. Ganesh Lall, wrapped in a white shawl, was sitting on his fourth floor balcony facing the place where the sun would rise. He was already absorbed in his devotions, chanting, making offerings, ringing his bell, and wielding his *bajra,* the brass symbol of the thunderbolt, representing the awesome power of the Tantric Buddha. I had no need to look out the window; I knew these sounds of early morning. I closed my eyes tighter. At 5:02 the crow community began to gossip about what had gone on during the night. Rumor spread in raucous waves until all the treetops were cawing. At 5:08 the jungle sparrows and magpie robins began to twitter. A few minutes later, as the pigeons started cooing softly in the eaves, I stirred at last. The sun rose while I made myself a cup of coffee and ate some finger-sized bananas though I knew I was cheating. The girls would go to the temple fasting. Perhaps they would not eat all day as a sacrifice to Ganesh. Many unmarried Newar girls fasted on Tuesdays, Ganesh's day. He was the god who could send a girl a good husband.

It was a cool October morning, that first time they took me to the Ganesh temple on the mountain. At six o'clock four little devotees waited outside my door. No, five. Chetana had her baby sister on her back. Shawls were pulled over their heads against the chill air. Their hands were full of brass *puja* trays and tin boxes of offerings. We started off, my little entourage talking and looking up at me like pretty bright-colored birds in pink and blue blouses and *punjabis*. Every other sentence began with "*Ho ki hoena, Miss?*" (Is it or isn't it, Miss?)

Once out of town our path ran between rice paddies. Some of the grain had already been cut with sickles and stacked in beige bundles against the mud wall of the next higher paddy. In others, the graceful drooping heads bent under their life-giving burden. In one paddy where the grain was not quite ripe, two men were tying the stalks together to keep the heavy rice out of the water. Small frogs splashed as we passed. White egrets posed among the stubble. "Look," said Chetana, and we paused to watch a black, red, gold, and chocolate grasshopper clinging to a dewy stem. Across a dip, banners of mist hid the village of Chandeshwari. Out of the mist, only the tiered brass pagoda tops could be seen, rising silhouetted against the jungled mountain—a strange mysterious vision of Nepal.

We kept having to crowd close to the edge of the path to let people pass. Many had finished their worship and were on their way back to Banepa. Some threw greetings to the girls as they passed. One woman asked softly who I was. "*Hamro Miss ho.*" (She is our Miss.) I smiled at Jiban who had answered. Many called me Root, or Rootji with the honorific added. To these charming children I was their Miss.

The path steepened and the water rushed over rocks. We entered a gorge where two streams joined. Here at the confluence there had once been a larger temple, and a finer one, than the small wood and plaster shrine where Ganesh stood opposite the brick rest-house. Cut and polished blocks of marble lay tumbled among the boulders of the torrent. Part of a wall and platform still remained, graced by a Shiva *lingam* and a small statue of Shiva's bull, Nandi. Here was the great Shiva keeping his son company; the gods, like the Nepalis themselves, are seldom alone.

"Renuka, tell me the story of Ganesh," I asked.

"Well, of course, he was the son of Shiva Mahadev and Parvati. All Nepal knows the tale of how he offended his terrible father who slashed off his head with his sword in anger. But Parvati, weeping, picked up her son's body and begged Shiva to bring him back to life. The great god, relenting said, 'So be it, I'll give him a head. The first one that comes along.' On his word an elephant wandered by."

"And," said Jiban, anxious to help, "Shiva cut off the elephant's head as neatly as he had Ganesh's and put it on the body of his son. Ganesh is the god who helps people over difficulties, which is why every *puja* begins with his name."

"He's the one who brings us husbands." Renuka looked down modestly.

And Shiva. I looked at the *lingam*, ancient fertility symbol used to represent Shiva. I thought of him sitting crosslegged on top of Mount Kailasa in the Western Himalaya. The new moon is caught in his long uncombed hair from which flows the water that becomes Ganga, the Ganges River, which waters thousands of miles of India. He is contemplating. Before his serenity, ages pass like minutes. His meditation maintains the world; but one day he will descend and dance the dance of destruction, which brings all things to an end.

My little girls knew some of this, but they did not suspect that Shiva went back at least to the time of Mohenjo Daro, before their Aryan ancestors came to India, back to the horned Lord of the Beasts. And that Ganesh had once been an elephant god of the ancients who worshipped strong and unpredictable things as men and women have done ever since they became human. In Nepal there is layer upon layer of understanding.

Above the platform with its humpbacked bull and *lingam*, the stream slowed in several small pools. By the highest a man squatted. He was almost naked. His head was shaved except for his *tupi*, the small lock that must never be cut, which men wear coiled and hidden in their hair. He was praying. In the central pool three middle-aged women bare to the waist were bathing. Four gray Asian crows hopped nearby. Renuka's beautifully chiseled little face smiled at me as she pulled a smock-like garment over her head. From under this she removed her blouse and punjabi trousers. Modestly, under their smocks, Jiban and Chetana and Indra were taking off their clothes.

"Miss, will you bathe?"

I took off my shoes and stockings and we all waded into the shallow, icy pool. I washed my hands and face and made motions at the ritual mouth cleaning. I dared not put the water in my mouth. All I drank must be boiled ten minutes and filtered. Even the clearest mountain brook can be full of the dread diseases still endemic in Nepal. Every trail becomes a latrine when it crosses a stream. (Water must be used to cleanse oneself, and all the indigenous bacteria and viruses float in the pure-looking water. Filtering is to take out the heavy burden of mica it bears.) I tried to look as though I were washing my mouth. It was sad that my Western sanitary knowledge must operate in such a lovely and holy spot, but I couldn't forget I'd had hepatitis and a few other troubles already.

Chetana unbraided her long hair and bent over to soap it. Indra shook hers out. I was surrounded by small water nymphs. Splashing themselves, washing their hair, becoming truly and ritually clean before they should approach the god. Laughing and shivering from the chill water, they came out to dry themselves. Holding a small mirror for each other they combed their hair, all the time giving me anxious smiles, checking to see that I was all right.

Then out came the boxes and they began to arrange their offerings on the shining brass *puja* trays in neat piles of red and yellow powder, cooked rice, pieces of banana, cucumber, guava. The girlish fingers mixed the colors with water, and reverently with intent faces Renuka and Jiban began to trace curving designs on the *lingam*, Shiva's phallus. Was the sexual caress they were giving it at all present in their minds? No, I thought, it is ritual and habit. But then I remembered that in Nepal the sexual embrace of the gods is endlessly portrayed to represent the strength of the gods and their power over life and fecundity as well as in the spiritual realm. The tip of Renuka's tongue was caught between her teeth as she concentrated on making her loops and circles perfect.

On top of the decorated *lingam* she placed fruit, a few red flower petals, two handmade wicks, and some holy water from a little bottle. The crows hopped nearer. One, with a loud caw, grabbed a piece of banana and gulped it.

Before we moved to the Ganesh temple Renuka put a red *tika* mark on my forehead and gave me rice to throw to the god. The Elephant-headed One was garlanded with pink cosmos and nearly smothered in offerings. We waited our turn while the young Brahman priest squatting by the god accepted the offerings of those before us, helped give them to Ganesh, and put his own share into a bag.

In our turn Chetana, Jiban, Renuka, Indra, and I all came up together. The girls anointed Ganesh's trunk, his paunch, his forehead, and his tusks with red powder. On his head and in front of him they placed flowers. They circled lighted wicks in the air and laid them at his feet with mounds of cooked rice and piles of fruit. I too put rice on his forehead and placed a half rupee, quickly retrieved by the priest, at his feet. Chetana handed me some flowers to give and a bunch of the kind of grass the Ganesh specially likes. She said, *"Tauknus,"* and indicated that I was to bend my head and touch the idol's feet. In respect for man's need of god, and for the mystery and power of the ancient ones, I did obeisance to this god of stone with his small elephant eyes. He helps to keep the world of Banepa running in its accustomed grooves, grooves a man (or a small girl) can understand and be secure in.

We retired from the presence, taking the loveliest of the dahlias we had given. They were *prasad* now, the leftovers of the gods, blessed by having been presented. Only now might we place them in our hair.

In the rest house beside the temple the girls paused to fasten the flowers, putting the largest and most beautiful into my hair. They made tiny balls of cooked rice and red powder and stuck them on our foreheads above the first *tika* from Shiva's *lingam*. Fresh flowers, *tikas*, shining clean hair. My little girls were pretty and gay. Their small breasts were just forming. Their earrings flashed as they talked. Chetana, daughter of the most prosperous shoe merchant in town, had blue tatoo marks on each arm for beauty.

Both she and Renuka had pink-eye in one eye, and when she took a bobby pin from her own hair to fasten the dahlia more securely in mine, I crossed my fingers, hoping I would not get lice. But it was only a passing shudder, a flick from that far away life I'd lived, a life centuries away from this mountain stream, the flower-decked god, the worshippers who had risen before dawn to prepare their offerings. Distant in space by half a world from this beautiful land of snows, terraced mountains, multi-tiered temples, filth, and fascination.

We started back. I saw the baby girl reach up to brush the rice-ball *tika* away. Immediately Jiban's hand caught the little arm and told the baby no, leave your *tika* there. I sympathized. I had caught my own hand about to brush away the strange-feeling substance on my forehead. The baby was being trained. Soon it would feel proper to her to wear whatever *tika* the occasion required.

On the way back the air was warm; the mists had gone from the rice paddies. Paddy birds were industriously fishing and a black fork-tailed drongo sat on a twig of bamboo. Beside the path is a rock that represents Parvati, Ganesh's mother. We tossed rice and the last of our flowers to her and to another three Shiva shrines as we passed.

It was eight-thirty. The girls bade me a smiling *"namaste"* and I went home to breakfast and preparation for school. They had told me they were going to fast all day.

The ten o'clock starting bell for school rang at eleven past. The *piun* had forgotten to wind the clock. It didn't much matter. There were only three of the twelve teachers there, and I was the only one who rose at the sound and went to class. Five of the 48 pupils were present in my classroom. Some wandered in later. My pretty little girls I clocked in at 10:31 with 13 minutes of the period left. I went on explaining the nervous system from a lurid chart. What would Renuka, Jiban, Chetana and Indra make of it?

The devotees of a god who can fit an elephant head on his son and make it grow—what need have they to know that the brain sends impulses through the nerves. Their life is complete and full. The days and years follow each other in god-decreed order. Man lives within that order.

Sometimes there is a slight change in the ancient pattern. A new flowered cloth may find its way north from India. Goods may arrive on a bus instead of in a *dhoka* on a man's back. A new way to show your prestige may be to send your daughter to school. But whatever is taught in the school won't affect your beliefs, or much dislocate your life. The elephant-headed Ganesh and his father on Mount Kailasa are the real things. They control the world.

If Nepal's thinking were black and white like ours, they couldn't need or use me at all. The saving grace is that contradictory things can happily coexist in their minds. Those who wanted to learn, like Yegya and Janak, and Siddi Bahadur, had room in their thinking for both science and faith. The moon is a goddess, but still men can land on her and take photographs and samples of the terrain as Neil Armstrong had done only a month before.

12

The Yelling Man

BESIDES THE LITTLE RED BOOK of *Chairman Mao's Thoughts*, the Communist Book Store in Banepa sold inexpensive books about the glories of Communism and the enlightened ways China was treating her minorities. My Nepali friends spoke of the Chinese "right" to Tibet. This was one of the few clues I had to their attitude to Communism. Since Peace Corps people were to be strictly apolitical, I never brought up the subject. How much Banepa knew of the brutal takeover in Lhasa, I was never sure. In Kathmandu there were many Tibetan refugees. Rumors about the flight of the Dalai Lama, and the repression of Buddhism must have been common. But closer, just across the highway, was a camp of Communist workers who had been building the Chinese Road from Kathmandu north to Tibet.

There were Communist meetings in Banepa, to which I was invited. A messenger would arrive with a flimsy slip of paper with my name and the time and place. My invitation was due to an incident a year before I came.

The Peace Corps Volunteers in Banepa before my immediate predecessor, an ill-fated butcher's daughter, had been two energetic, charming, and intelligent young Americans. I kept hearing about Barby and Susanne. They were much loved in the town. The Communists had held a meeting to which the whole of Banepa was invited, except the two American girls. The rest of the populace refused to go if Barby and Susanne were not invited too. The Communists gave way. So I, inheriting their mantle, was automatically invited this time.

My friend Krishna Prasad was one of the principal speakers. In his beautiful poet's voice he spoke in Newari all sorts of high-flown Communist principles. There were many more speeches, some drink like lemonade, and we adjourned. It seemed to be something to do. I could not see much excitement or enthusiasm in the audience.

Once in a while I would hear something like the story of Dick Nation, my nearest Peace Corps neighbor in Dhulikhel. He was helping with water and road projects and interestedly observed the big road the Communists were building with aid from China. The bridges on this road, where nothing but a trail had ever existed, were being made strong enough to support tanks. I never heard any Nepali mention that, but evidently our State Department knew it. I was given instructions that if Communist planes landed in Kathmandu for a takeover like the one in Tibet, I was not to try to go to Kathmandu and the American embassy, but to walk south over the Mahabharat Mountains and somehow find my way to India.

In general the Communists did not impinge much on my consciousness. But one afternoon I came back from visiting the little town of Bare Bise, at that time at the end of the passable part of the Chinese Road, slowly snaking its way toward Tibet. When I got back to town the first children who saw me rushed over to tell me the news. There had been a big communist meeting to memorialize the death of Ho Chi Minh the day before in Hanoi, a death of which I had not yet heard.

Their excitement came from the fact that I had been denounced at the meeting as an American Peace Corps Imperialist Spy. The cadre at the work camp had made an impassioned speech about the American aggression against Vietnam and about the viciousness of all Americans, of whom I was the closest representative. When I saw Krishna Prasad he told me it was not important. He gave me a reassuring smile and said, "Oh, it is just talk." After the excitement of telling me about it, I could see no hostility among the students who spoke to me.

But after dinner that night, after Om Bahadur had washed up the dishes and gone home, I heard strange noises in the courtyard. I looked out and saw a crowd. Some of them were staring at my windows. The rest were pressing around a young man in a Western suit with a black coat.

His voice rose and fell, almost screaming. He kept pointing at my house. I decided I didn't want to be seen to be watching. I drew back trying to catch his words. His voice rose to a shriek. I realized I was watching my first rabble-rousing, and I was the target. It was a frightening thought, a fearsome sound, a hysterical cry and roar. I ran downstairs to put a stronger bar across the already barred door. Then I crept back up to my third floor window to peer out. I found I was trembling.

The awful harangue shrilled and deepened below me. I couldn't see just who all the people were, but before long the shivering of my muscles lessened. What were they doing? It looked as though three men were pulling at the yelling man. Could they be trying to get him to leave? Yes, two men, one on each side, were taking him out toward the bazaar. The crowd followed him out, and the only looks that were directed at my windows were kind ones. My neighbors had refused to persecute me.

A few other Peace Corps volunteers met with harassment they were sure was communist inspired. The Chinese really believed we were spies. They knew what their own people would be doing if they could place volunteers all around Nepal in villages. But Nepal was not blind to the aspirations of its giant northern neighbor. It would not allow a Chinese "Peace Corps."

Later I found out that the would-be rabble-rouser lived in a room of the house attached to mine. He was a student being tutored and studying for the SLC exam. We used to pass each other in the bazaar but neither of us acknowledged the other's presence. Ram Bhakta spoke of him now and them in a derogatory way as the *karaune manche*, the yelling man. It was a more disapproving epithet than an American might think. Nepalis do not like loud voices or violent laughter.

In the end I seem to have won this confrontation, if such it could be called. One day there was a poetry reading, a popular kind of public gathering where many persons recited works of the great poets. The young would-be rabble-rouser came up to me as I sat gossiping in the cloth-merchant's shop and presented me with an invitation with my name handwritten on it. I smiled my thanks. I knew it was his apology.

13

The Eleven Match Fire

WHEN friends later asked me, "Did you enjoy your stay in Nepal?" I always wanted to explode, "No!" It was either wonderful and exhilarating or wrenching, depressing, unbearable. A polite mild word like enjoy had no place in that experience. I loved it or I could hardly bear it. A few pages of my notes show the gyrations of spirit I was always going through.

July 23, 1970

In the night I was awakened by the sound of something falling in the constant rain. This morning I discovered it was the wall around my ten square feet of back yard and the *charpi*. Om Bahadur had built it up and planted it with the red-flowered spiky Crown of Thorns in the days when he was my cook. I cleared the debris away from my little peach tree and from the bean I had planted in April which is now up to the third-story window. Both are still alive. While I was clearing away the mud, I saw Dilip's poor old grandmother come out of her door and lift her skirt to squat right there. Obviously she wears no underpants. I suppose none of the women do.

For my first class this morning there were 20 children present at the beginning. Am I changing their habits? Twenty is a better number than usual. Before the end of class nearly all were there. We were studying color and the prism. Toward the end we got to *indrani* (the rainbow). They all knew that the rainbow comes in, or—they all thought—after, the rain. But what other condition was necessary? No one could say. No one had noticed the sun must also be shining. We talked about it and made rainbows with the prism UNESCO had given the school.

My next period was free so I sat in the office. Fifteen minutes after the bell had rung Ram Bhakta drifted off to his class. Three other teachers followed him and went to their classes. In 15 minutes Ram Bhakta was back in the office, already finished with his "45 minutes" of instruction. Krishna Prasad told me he would bring my borrowed magnifying glass back to me after school. Gobinda read a bit of my *Time* magazine with me. Everyone else just sat. An hour later there was ten minutes of animation and they all laughed at some remark in Newari that I couldn't understand. Then apathetic quiet.

After school I lugged the microscope home for Biology Club. On the way, in the narrow cut between banks, I was nearly run over by a huge water buffalo with spreading horns. I grabbed hold of a plant and clung to the edge above him as the three-foot horns passed an inch from me. Later I found the plant had been a vicious nettle. Damn. My hand still hurts.

Coming down the bazaar I passed Ram Bhakta's house. In the shop that is the ground floor his littlest boy was running after his slightly older brother brandishing a *kukri*, the deadly knife that can behead a buffalo in one blow.

The other little boy was dueling with him, a bunch of straw in his hand. The man in charge rushed over and took away—the bunch of straw. I passed on down the bazaar, marveling.

The boys from the mountain village Wopi came right after school for Biology Club, but Lok Sudar and Dipac didn't show up though they ran a long way after me yesterday to tell me they were coming today. These Wopi boys keep finding and bringing me specimens of various plants and insects to identify. They all, Janak, Yegya, Rajah Ram, and Labakus, put in a good session examining various specimens under the microscope. My house is a better place to work than school. There I have to put the scope on a window ledge to get enough light.

Yegya and Janak say that after high school they will work on their farms. There is no possibility of going to college. I ask if they would go if their fathers could afford it. They both say a fervent yes. At present each of them is allowed an hour's play after school.

After they left I went to Gunga Devi's house, but she wasn't there though she had invited me. A few minutes later she showed up with a nice little picture book about Nepal to lend me. Ram Bhakta came by and said he would get the wall fixed for me tomorrow. I will wait and see.

July 24

I went out this morning to get some ferns for Jon, the Peace Corps Volunteer who has replaced Dick Nation in Dhulikel, for him to use in the new room he has been decorating. I came back with my hands full, kids clustering around as usual whenever I unlock my door. I came down in a few minutes to be sure I had locked the door again. I hadn't. The door to yard and *charpi* was unlocked, too, and the small volunteer peach tree I had been nursing along for four months was pulled up and gone.

It's like a wound to me every time they do one of these mean little tricks. Prakash, who is a close neighbor and seems one of my best friends, was here playing with the Spill and Spell game I carried back from the United States when I went home for my oldest son's wedding. He tells me spitefully that many of the children do not like me. When he leaves, two letters from the game are gone. Foolish little things to be depressed by, but everything is so hard to do, so hard to get, impossible to replace. I am always trying so hard. I am stretched nervously thin. I envy Jon; he is often on the verge of quitting and going home. He is free to do so. I am bound by my feeling of obligation to the few children who are really trying to learn.

These days I stay at school until the end of my last class, the next to last period, at 3:15. The muddy roads are too much to tackle twice a day. Krishna Prasad didn't come with the lens. I walked down the bazaar to get my Rising Nepal Newspaper. It wasn't there. "*Bholi* (tomorrow)," the shopkeeper told me. Darn. After walking through that stinking mud.

July 25

A big black sow has been lying beside my house for two days with her back broken. Her poor piglet has been trying to nurse. Much squealing from both of them. Every so often children throw stones at them. Just now the owner of the pig has appeared, tied her legs together, loaded her into the *dhoka*, which his son then helped him to hoist onto his back, and taken her away.

After watching from my high kitchen window, I start to fix breakfast. First I must light the little one-burner kerosene stove. I pick up a box of Nepali matches, and strike one. The too-thin wooden shaft splinters. I try another. That one doesn't have enough phosphorus on the end, and refuses to catch. Another. This one catches but the head goes flying off onto the floor. I strike them one after another. Finally one lights and I get the wick to catch. I count the ones that wouldn't light lying on the mudded floor around me. There are eleven of them. I'm deeply discouraged about my whole situation, and I say to myself, "That last one might as well have been a straw." I wish I could see an honorable way of getting out or of making things tolerable. But I can't. The best I can see is to worry along until December and the test that will be the last for me. At least there will be two glorious weeks of Dasain Holiday in October. Our planned Everest trek is Heaven to look forward to. I'm frantic to get back to my own kind of people.

August 25

Today was Gante Mangal. Before I went out to take a letter to register at the Post Office, I heard the boys calling *"he chani, hathi pani,"* or something like that. While I waited half an hour at the P.O. I found that they, the little boys, are going around to all the houses collecting straw. They string ropes across the street at every corner and collect *paisa* from all the passers-by. I had lots of small change ready for them. I'd gotten my letter registered at last, but there were no stamps that day. When there are I must watch the Postmaster cancel them or they may be stolen. As I went down the street toward home the kids told me the *paisa* were to buy materials for the *rachis* they are going to make. Jnan Kaji tells me the *rachis* is the ghost, or maybe the demon, at the crossroads.

Near the open area by the temples closest to my house, they are building our *rachis*, the one for our immediate neighborhood. Men are constructing it. First they shaped a straw body and put a *mala* of blossoms around his neck and another one of brightly colored rags. The children are yelling and running around with burning bundles of straw. I think of how horrified American mothers would rush to stop this. The Nepali mothers look on laughing. Everyone is having a fine time. Two little boys are sitting on the stone bull in front of the Mahadev Temple.

All the families across from the temple invite me to sit in their shops to watch. Prakash runs to put a white cushion down for me. When I take my camera out of my *jhola* I have a million requests for pictures. Every time I aim it, a half dozen little hams crowd in front of the lens. I finish a roll of film and have to change just as the *rachis* is getting his head. It is a winnowing tray with features painted on it. Another tray cut in half makes his two ears. At this point all the women and girls who have been watching suddenly disappear. The men now produce the final touch, two grapefruit attached on either side of a long fruit ending in a red ball. From this dangles a thin strip of white cloth. This is more realism than I was expecting, but they are holding up the process waiting for me to change film. At this climactic moment the film doesn't mesh with the ratchet of my old Leica. I have to cut the end off and start loading all over while everyone waits for me. As soon as I am ready (and also apprehensively thinking I should have retreated with the other females) they lead me around in front of the *rachis*. He has several erections for the camera, which is now committed to recording the proceedings. Or should I leave before things go even further?

Subhadra, the boy who swallowed his notes when I caught him cheating at school, runs by with a huge heart-shaped leaf two-and-a-half feet long. He is on his way to the *rachis* belonging to the next neighborhood crossroad. I am caught. I must see what will happen now.

Our *rachis* starts up the street. Theirs, with the leaf appropriately painted with red lines and covering the lower half of her body, is braced to meet him. Encounter. Encounter after encounter. Finally he gets her down and throws himself on top of her.

Then our men rush the two *rachis* up the bazaar. The boys all carry flaring torches. Everyone is yelling. Great commotion and excitement as they dash past other *rachis* belonging to other neighborhoods. Clear through town they run, past the *pokhri* at the far end of the bazaar and on to the burning *ghat* by the river. There the *rachis* are

Our neighborhood's male demon, all assembled and decorated in the last hour and a half, ready to march up the bazaar in search of conquest.

ceremonially cremated. Escorted by Dilip, I watched. I was glad I couldn't understand the Newari words the men kept calling out—answered each one by the boys in yelling chorus.

At the *pokhri* I leave and go up to my knoll. I spend a long time watching smoke from funeral pyres of other *rachis* rising all over the valley. Two processions of men and boys stream out of Banepa, the one I had just left, and one going out from Wokutol toward Chandeshwari.

Evening, and the crows making the racket they are named for. *Kagh! Kagh!* Beautiful contours of our valley. One late-working man hoeing his terrace. The Newari religion does not allow plowing. Hundreds of egrets, sailing to their roosts in flights of one to a dozen, wing in from far away to the tall trees of Banepa. Peace and beauty!

I'd almost forgotten that the man who was to fix the wall, as Ram Bhakta had promised, didn't show up.

One last flight of egrets, graceful white forms against the dark green lower hills. I see again that first flight Howard and I watched from the old palace, so long ago. Sudden agony twists me.

August 26

Early this morning I went again with the little girls on the Tuesday pilgrimage to the Ganesh temple by the streams' confluence. This time the girls had *me* make the offerings. If I make a gesture wrong, or do things out of order everyone laughs, but in kindly fashion. They help me. We came back with flowers in our hair and big *tikas*.

What did the men who joined the Foreign Legion seek? They and the Peace Corps Volunteers are alike. Life had turned sour and impossible at home. Or they just had nothing special they wanted to do there. They were seeking answers. Not positive answers so much as to get away from the place where there was no answer. Maybe all they would find were new questions.

After school Lok Sudar, who had asked to come and see me, didn't come, so I had time to pick a whole peck of beans by leaning out my third-story window. Jack's beanstalk was nothing. The little girls popped in to say, "*Miss, na pakaunus.* (Don't cook). We will come for you for dinner." However, Jnan Kaji had said he was coming, so I made some snacks to give him with tea. He never came, but Jon dropped by to tell me he couldn't come tomorrow, so he and I ate the snacks and drank a glass of Three Tigers whiskey to the health of my new first grandchild, my middle son's son.

Jon left at seven and Renuka, Jiban, Indra, and Chetana came for me. We went to Jiban's house where they had a fine meal ready, including yoghurt mixed with water (unboiled, of course). Hope I survive. Everyone else was shut out and we had a good dinner together. Then they opened the door and let in about 10 younger brothers and sisters, who were supposed to dance for me, but never quite made it. Giggles and shyness. I danced a little trying to encourage them. They sang a song. After a while I said "*Namaste*" and left, but Renuka insisted on taking me to see her mother and father for a few minutes to look at snapshots, very dim, in which I had to try to recognize all the family. Then to my house where the girls came in and started reading my books. As they left Lok Sudar came, but so did Bichisarma, the priest from next door with his five-year-old son. Bichisarma of course took precedence. He had been here two evenings ago when the Conversation Club met. He had hoped we were writing English, had printed out the alphabet in capitals, and I had shown him the small letters. Tonight he printed the capital letters again. What he really wanted this time was to ask if his small son could sit in at my tenth grade class at the high school and listen. I could visualize a mile long row of little "listeners" all the way down the hill to Banepa.

I finally eased them out, my lovely day having turned too complicated to be much fun anymore. I got one sentence typed and the fuse to my light bulb blew. This is the third time it has blown in two days, but when I try to tell the tailor that it is his wiring that is faulty he just acts pitiful and says that every other house's light is on.

August 27

The story about the light is this: the tailor, one of the tenants in the house attached to mine, spends his days sitting cross-legged on the ground floor in front of his hand-operated sewing machine. He always works until the daylight is gone, trying to see to stretch out his working time. I worried about him and offered to let him attach a wire to my electricity for a light to save his eyes. He was grateful and made good use of the one bulb that he got installed in one of the two rooms his family lives in.

But something has gone wrong, and my fuse keeps blowing. As I went out this morning the tailor's wife was at the door. I told her there must be a short in her wiring that was blowing my fuses. No, she said, the trouble was the other part of the house. I didn't know that while I was away two other apartments in the house had hooked on to my electricity! It seems that Ram Bhakta had told them they could. He had at first said that they must ask me, but then told them to go ahead and attach to the tailor's wire.

One of the two new wires was going to the *karaune manche* (the young communist who gave the rabble-rousing speech in front of my house). He is now living there and teaching at a small elementary school up near

Tindada while studying at night for his SLC exam. The other is Bichisarma's, whom Ram Bhakta says they would call a *gurju*, a family priest of Buddhist Newars. It seems he also is studying for the SLC.

Ram Bhakta and I go over this for three-quarters of an hour with no smallest meeting of minds. My point is that the wires he told people they could attach are blowing fuses and making my light useless, so I can't work. His point is that they are studying for the SLC. We never understand each other's viewpoint. To all of them I am a resource to be used, even if only between blown fuses. But I must have my light. (It turned out to take an exhausting struggle of months before I could arrange all this between me, them, and the electric company.)

Early morning. I met the butcher coming down the street with empty hands. Or rather empty shoulders, for butchers always carry their wares in two baskets yoked across their shoulders. Today is *ekadasi* (the eleventh day) and it is forbidden to cut. To butcher, that is.

11:00 a.m. Tired after the morning classes. Went to the Clarks' for a delicious lunch and got home just at 2:00, when I had invited several women to come and learn how to can fruits. What a horrid fiasco. They came and peeled *naspati* while the water boiled to sterilize the bottles. But when I started to show Ganesh Maya the ones I had tried the system out on, I found that all were moldy. These Nepali, or Indian, bottles do not seal, it seems. Perhaps the rubbers are too thin to stand boiling. I can't think of any other possible mistake. I am horribly embarrassed. I must tell them all that I cannot do what I promised. Oh, dear! I took one up to Wopi, too! As a present for Yegya's mother.

I'm afraid the demonstration would have been a mess

even if the jars had been all right. I asked them to speak
Nepali so I could understand, and that put a damper on
the day. Dhana Maya said, "But when you meet your
friends you want to talk to them." Talking Nepali to me
was too much trouble. Krishna Maya had left before that.
We, mostly I, put the *naspati* through the food mill, then
before the processing Gunga Devi and Ganesh Maya both
left after poking around my kitchen a bit and turning on
and leaving the tap of my filter running so that the
precious water carried up to this fourth floor kitchen was
gone just when there was a big mess to clean up. No one
stayed to see the processing, but what difference did it
make when one cannot get jars with seals in Nepal? I ate a
horrid supper of horse beans and went up to my knoll to
watch the sunset. After ten lovely solitary minutes the
mother of the girl who carries water up to the school came
to sit beside me.

I was trying to forget the sorry history of this canning
lesson. For a year Ram Bhakta had begged me to teach his
mother how to can. I wrote home to Sears for jars for
canning. Months later I had their letter saying they could
not ship jars to Nepal. Ram Bhakta told me The Blue
Bucket, the most Westernized store in Kathmandu, had
canning jars. I bought five to try out and processed a trial
batch. When I turned the jars upside down to test the seal,
they seemed all right. I bought ten more and carried the
fragile things home in my *jhola* on the bus. Bought *naspati*
and sugar, went around to half a dozen women's homes to
invite them to come. I had talked the whole project over
with Ram Bhakta's mother before I invited anyone else.

Yesterday I said to him, "Ram Bhakta, your mother
didn't come to the canning you and she asked for." He
waved his hands airily in the how-can-I-help-it gesture.
Later I found that a nephew had died in Kathmandu and,

of course, she had to go there. But no one told me.

A year's effort ends in nothing but disaster. I look ridiculous. No one guesses how hard I tried.

Oh, Howard, how I miss you, long for you. What am I doing here?

14

The Intolerant God

THE DOCTOR DIRECTOR'S WIFE, David's mother, got up off her knees and looked at her eldest child. Her expression trembled between stern admonition and patient smile. She shook her head at David. He had resumed his seat too quickly, popped up off his knees like a spring released. And the question he had asked, as the faces of the others made clear, was unthinkable. David sighed and shifted in his chair so he could no longer watch the torches bobbing past the wall of the Mission compound. They were the flares of another of the innumerable religious processions on its way to the temples of Chandeshwari.

The Mission staff was holding its Monday night prayer meeting in the walled hospital enclosure across the valley from Banepa. The Director and his wife, his elder sister, a younger American couple who assisted him, an Indian Doctor and his wife, the Indian accountant, Indian nurses. There were no Nepalis on the staff. Though the hospital had been there for nine years, conversion had been disappointingly slow, and they would have no one on the staff not belonging to their Seventh Day Adventist Church. The only Nepali present was Bhaju Ram, a new convert and a protege of the doctor's sister, who had taken him under her wing.

All of them, the American blue eyes and the Indian black ones, stared grimly at David. His mother would have liked to rescue her son, but his question, "Could a Hindu go to Heaven?" was astonishing. Most people, even those who called them-selves Christians, would never go to Heaven.

99

Outside the compound, in all of Nepal, a myriad of gods dwelt together in amity. Some were ferocious, some beneficent, or both by turns in their different aspects. One thing they all had in common was a tolerance and respect for each other. Buddha shared his temple with a dozen Hindu gods and godlings. The great Shiva was as generous. Laxmi and Kali, Narayan and Ganesh and numinous stones whose indwelling divinity's name had been lost to memory, shared honors with each other. In the Buddhist temple compound at the full moon of Purnima, a group of Buddhist worshippers would be intoning Buddhist chants, while, in complement to them, Hindus in another corner sang their own mantras, each group accompanied by its own musicians. Each group felt enhanced by the presence of the other. Both Buddhist and Hindu. Luckily, Nepal had practically none of the Islamic sects that rent India into bloody parts after its independence.

Inside the walled hospital grounds there was only one god, the Jehova of one of Christianity's strictest sects. He had said, "Thou shalt have no other gods but me." The Adventists knew his advent was near. He was coming, a god of wrath, a jealous god, to destroy all abominations, which meant all the world's people who did not worship by the True Light they alone followed. He would blast all people outside the sect. Heaven was only for the elite, the believers, the Seventh Day Adventists.

The boy who had asked the question about heaven stared back at the others, abashed. "I meant someone like Ganesh Lall, down in Banepa, who prays all the time. Or Bim Bahadur. He ran into the burning house and saved his little son. Couldn't *they* go to Heaven?"

The fat, almost black Indian accountant exploded. His short arms waved, his round face puckered, his high-pitched voice which was seldom silent, whined and snorted. "No! They are heathens. They are confirmed in sin and error. Jesus said, 'Believe on me and ye shall be saved'. Those who believe, only those who know the truth as we do, they are the only ones who shall not burn in Hellfire Everlasting!"

The Director smiled his patient, conciliator's smile. "Perhaps it would be kinder to say that Heaven is not the place for them. It will be thronged with the righteous."

His wife was still thinking of her son's question. Ganesh Lall she hadn't heard of, but she had seen Bim Bahadur because his baby had been burned badly enough to be kept in the hospital for a month. Of course his father had stayed to cook for him because he must not eat food cooked by a lower-caste person. She knew Bim was a mild man and a loving father.

"I think," she said at last, "that Hindus wouldn't feel at home in Heaven. A few *very good* ones might enter, perhaps."

A look of almost-concealed relief came over the face of Bhaju Ram. He thought uncomfortably of his grandfather, father, brother and sisters. He had broken with them, but he loved them still.

The Indian doctor and the assistant began to protest, but the Director waved them aside and went on to the next part of the lesson. "Repentance of sins is imperative. Unless we repent we shall not go to Heaven. The Bible tells us so."

Here there was no possible argument. His sister stood up and repented of not being patient enough with the missionaries' children she was teaching, David, Patricia, and Samuel. The Director repented of staying up too late to read a religious book when he should have been sleeping to prepare himself for the next day's work. His wife had forgotten and started to write a letter on Saturday, the Sabbath.

I felt I really shouldn't be there, though I had been specially invited by these kind people who had always been good friends to me. I knew I shouldn't speak. But I tried to put my question gently. "If you repent of those things, what about . . . your missionary work? How do you reconcile yourselves to breaking the law of the country which is your host? It's against the law to convert people, yet you have a hundred children coming up here for Sabbath School."

There was no uneasiness in the answer. "We hold Sabbath School in our own home for ourselves. If the Nepalis want to come they may."

The assistant spoke, a fanatic fire in his blue eyes. "We are here to heal and cure the people. Often a man who is ill and in trouble may need the Savior and Redeemer without knowing what he wants. We offer the Light! If it is the soul which is ill, we may save it! What more glorious act than to give a heathen a chance to see Christ face to face! As true believers do."

Around me was the only Western enclave in all our vast valley. Here alone was there running water in kitchen and bathroom. Here there was refrigerator and a big cooking stove, a washing machine, a freezer, a furnace to heat the whole house, a piano. Unheard of, undreamed of luxuries. What a powerful god it must be who could provide all these things to his worshippers. Suddenly I wondered how the Nepalis looked at me. I lived almost the way they did. Might this be because I respected Buddha, and Shiva, Ganesh and Narayan? A Nepali must be impressed when faced by a god worshipped by rich, well-fed, dedicated followers who, moreover, ran a hospital to minister to Nepali illnesses.

Most Nepalis, nevertheless, held true to their own way. Even in India, it was mostly the untouchables, people who were almost excluded from their own culture, who became Christian. But more were converting these days. Could the ancient gods continue to withstand the combination of prosperity, technology, and Christianity?

The Adventists felt positive that they were devoting their lives to the greatest of causes, but believing that almost everything the Nepalis did and thought was wrong, they naturally did not understand them too well.

The Director's wife once said to me, "They don't seem at all embarrassed by their religion." She told me as a cute story that the day before one of their former doctors returned to the United States he went all over Banepa "making people happy" by taking pictures of them—with an empty camera. He never thought of the waiting for pictures that didn't come and the plans Banepa people had made around them. They still said to me proudly, "The doctor is going to send me my picture." They loved and desired photographs. If, on a packed bus, I happened to open a letter with a snap-shot enclosed, someone was sure to reach for it. It would be passed around so that each man, woman, and child, jammed together as they were, could examine it. The people of Banepa still hoped for those promised photographs.

The assistant gave puppet plays to teach the Nepalis, who love cigarettes, not to smoke. But the villain of the piece was a rascally tiger, and the heroine was a woman who kept always doing the right thing and putting out cigarettes. Of course, the Nepalis loved the tiger and hated the goody-goody woman.

But Nepalis are tolerant. They came to Sabbath School. They were grateful for the hospital. The Adventist Jesus was another god, and all gods are to be respected.

And yet—the Nepalis knew that all Westerners, those fortunate people with all sorts of much-to-be-desired possessions, worshipped gods unlike the great Shiva, and Narayan and Bhairava. Some doubts entered young minds. Tika Bhakta once said to me, "Sometime I might try eating cow." He looked both daring and frightened as he said it.

A Kathmandu man, who worked for the British Embassy, telling me of the dread god Pachali Bhairab, maintained he did not believe in him. But he shivered, and added, "Nevertheless he is very terrifying."

I myself was terrified for the Nepali way of life—which is not separable from their religious view of the world. One night I saw some other missionaries operating. These were not my kind neighbors. There were several European evangelistic groups in Nepal under other guises, ostensibly running book stores, or studying linguistics, or offering some social service, but I heard them whisper "Operation Mobilization," meaning the converting of Nepalis.

We were at the home of a woman I had barely met. I thought I had been invited just to dinner. (One of the worst I ever ate: luke-warm thin soup, bread, no butter, limp beans, fried lumps of some fish, *naspati* in a horrid pink sauce.)

After this repast we went into the next room and heard a sermon. Jesus died for *you*. It was Sunday night (these were not Seventh Day Adventists). After the sermon each missionary went to and grabbed—there was no other word for it—one Nepali and started working on him. "You dare not ignore the death of Jesus on the cross. He died for your salvation. Believe on him or you will surely go to Hell." I slunk away.

15

The Oil Pressers

THE PEACE CORPS TEACHER who preceded me in Banepa had a miserable time of it. Her father had been a perfectly respectable butcher in Madison, Wisconsin and she had said so. This was suicidal in a Hindu society. To any Hindu a butcher is an untouchable, and the people of Banepa naturally shrank from her. She stayed two months and then ran off with an Indian she had met in Kathmandu. The son of a butcher.

Theoretically, I was as much of an outcaste as she, since neither of us belonged to any Hindu caste. But my father was a university professor and my grandfather had been a Lutheran minister, so though I was without caste, the people of Banepa tolerantly felt that in my own country I must be some dim approximation of a Brahman.

In Nepal caste determines all of your passage through life. It determines whom you can eat rice with, can accept water from, touch, or marry. I was a strange anomaly. Not only did I have no caste; people were not even sure of my sex (or that of any Western woman). Women wore long dresses. We didn't. They wore big earrings and, often, nose rings. We didn't. Our earrings were much more like those small single ones men and boys wore. Women had long hair. We didn't.

Figures didn't seem to count. Though mine is quite unequivocal, I remember a day on the bus to Kathmandu as one of several experiences. The couple in front of me craned around to talk. After several minutes of chatting about the weather and crops, they turned back and I heard the wife say, *"Aimai ho."* (It's a woman.)

Since I had no fixed place in their society, I was free to have acquaintances of all kinds and castes. One of the castes from which I knew many people was the Manandhars. It began with Jnan Kaji Manandhar, an English teacher at the High School. Unlike Rajendra, the other English teacher, Jnan Kaji spoke English easily and liked to speak it. He was one of the few teachers who became a friend. Most of them shied away from my strangeness.

There were a lot of Manandhars in Banepa. By tradition they were pressers of oil and Jnan Kaji's family owned an old press for making mustard oil. In the ranking of castes, they are about the lowest of the "clean castes." It is even rumored that they were not always a clean caste, but ranked among the butchers and barbers whose touch was pollution to any upper caste. Even now the Manandhars are not of exalted caste, yet their status is good because they are hard-working and well-off and an ambitious group. Jnan Kaji was the first Manandhar in our valley to be educated, and his son and some of the other youngsters are being helped to go further than he. When the Headmaster chose eight top pupils to be in my English Club three of them were Manandhars.

Jnan Kaji's father was an exceptional man and the head or *kaji*, as the Manandhars called it, of the caste. He had written and produced for the town many plays from the old mantras. He was believed to have power over ghosts. Stories were told me of how he drove evil spirits from the bodies of their victims. He always gave me very respectful *namaste* with his joined hands on his forehead. One of my great regrets was that I did not speak Newari so that I could have talked to him, for he spoke no Nepali or English. In a land where religion was as pervasive as breathing, the Manandhars seemed especially devout. They were a Buddhist caste, but in Nepal the Buddhist and Hindu religions were so tolerantly intertwined that when I asked Jnan Kaji what the differences were, he answered, "There is no difference. It just depends on what you were born."

In Nepali community festivals, different castes, sometimes even untouchables, have special duties to perform. The Manandhars have many such responsibilities. It is they who must go to the forest to select a special tree, trim it into a pillar, and erect it in Hanuman Dhoka, Kathmandu's ceremonial center, for the great Indra Jatra, when the Living Goddess comes forth from her secluded house and is paraded through the city. They do the same for the important festival of Bisket in Bhaktepur, another of the Malla royal cities in the days of Newar rule. But most important to the Manandhars is the month of their *puja* of Sringabheri which falls in late summer.

One August afternoon, after three days of monsoon rain, I heard a call at my door. Jnan Kaji's nephew, Chakra Kaji, had been sent with a message. I must come back with him to the family house. We walked through the steady stream that flowed over the random stones and bricks of the bazaar street. In front of the cloth merchant's house a scrawny black hen was squawking and ruffling herself up. Trying to keep a pig away from her solitary baby chick, she made desperate rushes at the grunting pig. A wet gray crow was pecking at some manure. We splashed along past shrines, and shops, and houses.

At Jnan Kaji's the musicians I'd seen that morning, on their way to the temple of Chandeshwari, were on the second floor looking over their instruments. On the third floor stood a newly made altar. There were many flowers and small brass lamps on the floor in front of a row of people sitting cross-legged. All along the upper part of the wall ran a series of sacred pictures: brightly colored gods and goddesses. Jnan Kaji took me around to tell me their stories—Ram, the great hero of the Ramayana, Sita his wife, the great god Shiva and his wife Parvati, their son

Banepa bazaar in monsoon season.

the Elephant-headed Ganesh, and Buddha in several of his aspects. Hindu and Buddhist gods hobnobbing in amity.

I was introduced for the first time to Jnan Kaji's respected father and his two dimpled and charming daughters. The room was full of Manandhars, most of whom gave me *namaste* as I looked around. They were ranged around the walls, and we had been stumbling among them as Jnan Kaji showed me the pictures. Each one had in front of him a board on which he was making small stupa-shapes from black clay forced into little brass molds. Everyone had a brass lamp and containers for oil and water and offerings of food and flowers. A priest came in and seated himself on a chair in the center of the room. He began to intone in Newari—long lists by the sound of it. Perhaps he was saying the names of the gods or would it have been the history of Buddha's life?

This was the beginning of a month-long ceremony, and the musicians who had waked me that morning with blasts from their horns and conch shells had been part of it. Jnan Kaji's plump face topped by curly black hair smiled at me. He began to explain again. There was a look of pride in his eyes, a shine of love and devotion to his gods and his people.

Strong men, he told me, had gone to the river bank and brought back loads of the black clay. Our river was holy as all rivers and streams are holy. If it is possible for a Newar to be carried to a river to die with his feet in the flowing water he is taken there so that his spirit can go more directly to Yama's house.

Now the Manandhar clan was engaged in turning the clay into thousands of the tiny black stupa-shapes that they called Buddhas. As the priest intoned they threw rice or flowers, poured oil, or chanted responses, never pausing more than a moment in the making of the black clay Buddhas, each with a few grains of rice pressed into it.

I looked around and saw faces of some of my students,

Bhuban, son of Jnan Kaji, and Raj Bhai, who were two of the best students. It was almost 10 o'clock, time for classes to begin, but I knew they would not be at school this morning. Nor would Jnan Kaji be there to teach, not until the *puja* was over at about noon. Jnan Kaji, though, in the accepted manner, would sign in as if he had been there all day. School had only to do with temporal matters, and this worship with eternal ones.

Every day for a month Sringabheri was celebrated in the Kaji's house. More Manandhars gathered until there was no room for them around the walls. So they simply broke a hole through into the next house, which happened to belong to the Kaji's brother. Next day when I came for an early visit I found a new loop added to the row of worshipers extending through the hole in the wall and around the walls of the room in the next house. Each person was sitting in front of a little lamp, making Buddhas, throwing flowers and rice, and performing all the other rituals in time to the chanting of the priest. It was strange to see the group through the rough hole because the floor of that room was two feet higher than the one I stood in.

I always came long before school and left in time to meet my first class at ten even though I knew the *piun* would ring the bell when he saw me enter my room, and that mine would be the only class to start.

Jnan Kaji often invited me to his house and many times took me around Banepa showing me the old temples and shrines while telling me old stories or quoting Shakespeare, which he loved and was proud of knowing. Sometimes he would visit me at home and I would serve him sweet spicy Nepali tea and biscuit. At his house I would be given tea and *chura*, the flattened rice made by the pounding that I had thought must be an electric pump that first morning when my senses had not yet become attuned to the local conditions and activities. Sometimes his little daughter would bring me a small aluminum plate with a soft-fried egg. This tested my not-very-well-learned skill at eating with my right hand. Especially if I had no *chura* to mix the runny egg with, I could not do it neatly. Jnan Kaji could.

We would be eating in the small room of the house that was Jnan Kaji's and his wife's—the only part of the house that was theirs. We would sit on the mat where they slept at night, the mosquito net rolled up above our heads. The rest of the house was communal. This room belonged only to the eldest son. That was the way all households were organized. It was the natural way life should be lived.

I asked no question but he told me how fine it was to live in an extended family, where everybody helped each other in everything. He could afford to teach school on the small salary because his home was here where they all shared.

I knew that the reason for the pressing invitation to the Sringabheri rituals was so that I could photograph them and I came as often as I could. The climax began one night at the end of the month.

Again Chakra Kaji came for me. This time I found the altar on the third floor enlarged and topped with a two-foot-high black mud stupa. Beside it sat the priest, huddled over a small fire burning on the mud floor. Round and round the fire and stupa paraded all the Manandhars I had come to know over this month of worship. I joined the line at the gesture of one of the women. All of them tossed rice into the fire and at the black mud stupa that they called a Buddha. In a bin beside it were all the thousands of small Buddhas they had made from the sacred river mud. In my ignorance I had brought no rice so I began to throw small coins. On the second round, without missing a beat of the chant, Chandra Devi behind me slipped me a handful of rice.

Next morning when I went to the Kaji's house men were just finishing painting the last of five Bhodisatvas around the doorway and two small *raths* were being built and decorated. In the afternoon all the preparations ended in a great procession through the main street of Banepa down to the river below town. Boys ran in front giving offerings of small cakes to all the people of Banepa who lined the street. After them came the musicians with conch and drum and pipes. The *raths* followed, escorted by the Kaji with a sacred gourd, five fasting women, and a man bearing flaming lamps on his head and shoulders. Behind them came all the Manandhars following the music and a dozen men carrying great baskets full of the offerings of small Buddhas they had made. Jnan Kaji motioned to me to join in.

Through the bazaar we went and down to the river. I had my camera ready for whatever ceremony was to occur, but I jumped in amazement when most of the men waded into the river and it suddenly exploded in what looked like the biggest water fight in history. That was the end. The sacred mud had been formed into Buddhas imbued with spirit by the rice grains put into them. Now they were returned to holy nature in the sacred river. The circular oneness of the world had been reaffirmed once again. It was over and we went home. For the whole Manandhar caste it had been a fulfillment and an intensification of their own identity and values.

There were religious festivals of some kind every week and the daily worship in the home shrines and all the temples, but this month was a special time of joy for Manandhars. Each caste had days and rituals of its own. They were the vital color and religious substance of life.

The Sakya caste (goldsmiths) also celebrates the sacred month of Buddha. Their red Buddhas parade and are worshiped. Note the peephole for the man supplying motive power.

16

On Top Of A Sacred Mountain

IN A COMMUNITY where each individual had his own special, universally understood, niche from birth, it must have taken real courage to be a friend to someone so strange to Banepa as I was. My whole view of the world was fundamentally different from theirs. I was white, a Westerner, neither Hindu nor Buddhist. Ritually I was an unclean person in their world, yet they were generous to me and very kind.

They could never reconcile themselves to the fact that I lived alone. Had I no sons? That was perhaps the strangest thing about me—the fact that I was alone. I not only had left my sons to come to Nepal. I didn't want someone always with me. Sometimes I would not let visitors enter. My need for privacy was incomprehensible to them. One man asked me if his little daughter could watch me bathe so she could learn the Western way. My first maid, the one who was afraid of going home after dark because of the leopards, asked if I wouldn't like to have her sleep in my bed. A group would jostle me to look over my shoulder as I read. Nepalis lived their lives close, very close, to each other.

Another barrier was that I was always so tight with tension within myself, so conscious of the shortcomings of my Nepali. I knew I made many mistakes, knew there was much I didn't understand. I felt adrift in a strange culture.

And, too, there was the pain of losing Howard, an ache that never left me. If only I could have relaxed, and enjoyed wholeheartedly the friendliness so freely offered. The tight knot of uncertainty and loneliness was something I kept trying to overcome. I felt pressed on all sides by all the people, all the difficulties, all the things I might not be understanding.

Yet I loved the country. I delighted in its many beauties, and I loved the people. It seems strange to say I loved them and yet tried to hold them off. But it was so. The fact that there were so many of them always close by made me feel suffocated. I needed privacy, which was not an entity they had any understanding of. I don't believe any of them ever wished to be alone, except holy men who spent hours at their devotions.

On festival days everyone in the town was joyful. Those were the times I felt nearest to them. They wanted me to share and admire. At festivals I enjoyed everything, was fascinated by them all. They would make room for me at the front of the crowd, tell me what was going on. I remember the Buddhist festival when the red Buddha of the Sakya caste had been paraded around Banepa. He had come to rest in the lower bazaar. My student Prakash insisted on taking me into the house opposite where, above the people, I could watch the priest and the worshippers bringing offerings to the god in his gold jewelry and fresh flower decorations.

Prakash took me through dark rooms and up a black narrow staircase, saying "*Aunuhos, aunuhos*," as he led me to the front room overlooking the street. Taro and Bhusan followed and we all looked down on the lights and color of the worshippers bringing their offerings in shining brass bowls. A woman came into the room, obviously the lady of the house. She stared at me in amazement, an unexpected interloper in her home. Almost immediately she recovered and gave me a sweet smile and a *namaste* and a cordial invitation to enjoy her room.

I remember so many faces, and all of them smiling. One was Dilip's. He was about three feet tall it seemed, and very dark-skinned. He lived in the house to the right of mine, into whose courtyard I looked when, of an evening, I climbed up to my kitchen window to watch the white egrets returning to roost. Dilip was in my sixth grade class and was one of the boys who came to my house to play with the basketball, or the crayons and paper, or the simple little games I had.

Dilip's elder sister, Sushila, was one of the good students in tenth grade and, when I was finally persuaded to take a few children for an English Conversation Club, she was one of the two girls in it. I had held out against teaching any English. After all, I was there to teach science and I was trying so desperately to learn Nepali well that I had no time for English. But I finally gave in and that group of eight became one of my joys.

They came to my house in the evening, and we played games, chatted, and had a good time in English. Though they had studied English in school for years, they were sadly unprepared. They needed much more study and work. One sound they could not make was the English *th*. We kept practicing. Especially we practiced my name, but I was Root to the end.

It was with that group that I spent one of my loveliest days in Nepal. They had begged me to go on a picnic to Nam Buddha, a shrine on a mountaintop half a day's walk away. I promised that I would come back early from my Christmas vacation, so it was the third of January when they came to my house to prepare the food, as they had begged me to let them do.

I had returned with a miserable cold, but I knew how they looked forward to the day, so I let them come. Although my provisions and utensils were meagre and included nothing that couldn't be bought in Banepa or carried out in a string bag on the bus from Kathmandu, my students found my kitchen irresistibly odd. They were anxious to use my five-tiered aluminum picnic container, and to see how I lived. The first thing they did was to run out to the bazaar for a lot of spices I had never considered necessary. Then all the spices, especially ginger root, red pepper, and cumin, had to be ground and pounded vigorously. They peeled, and chopped and cooked. Raj Bhai swept the floor clean.

They planned everything. We must take the Chinese propaganda magazine with its glossy pictures for plates. We must take my flashlight and my camera and my thermos bottle, all novelties in Banepa. All these went into *jholas* which we would carry over our shoulders. They packed rice and various curries and pickles into the aluminum bowls and locked them together one on top of the other. We were prepared.

Next morning they were at my house at six o'clock: Bhuban Manandhar, Raj Bhai Manandhar, Bikram Sakya, Lok Sudar Bhaila, Tika Bhakta Bhocki Bhoya, Syam Mhaske. The two girls were too shy to come with us. By Banepa standards that would have been improper, though classes with boys were reluctantly sanctioned and they had been enjoying coming to my house.

There was frost on the ground glistening in the dim light. We started off on a valley trail that I had never taken. Tika Bhakta carried my camera, Raj Bhai the binoculars. We crossed the river on a jeepable bridge but from there on we took a foot trail. A man and woman carrying loads in *dhokas* supported by headstraps were followed by three ragged children clutching shawls over their heads. All of them were barefoot, and as they passed I looked at the feet of my boys. Raj Bhai wore rubber thong sandals; the others wore tennis shoes except Bikram, the son of a goldsmith. He wore good leather shoes.

The light was beginning to brighten. We hurried up the rising path. A little way ahead, the boys told me, we would climb to the pass where we could see the *himals*. I wanted badly to see the rosy glow of sunrise on them from this new angle. The white line of peaks and domes against the sky was always breathtaking and always different. We reached the pass; before us was their glorious beauty. I stood and watched until the pink paled, faded, and finally turned white and gleaming.

We stopped for a while in a roadside house that belonged to a distant cousin of Tika Bhakta's. He had a message to give them, and they insisted on giving us tea and *chura*. After that the trail began to climb around a shoulder of the little mountain we were on. In the dooryards of the scattered, mud-covered thatched houses, people squatted in the sun, absorbing every bit of heat.

The white *himals* showed in the distance. Rounded brown

hills and small mountains surrounded us. All that weren't terraced fields had been pasture for years, and the water buffaloes and cattle had worn innumerable criss-crossed paths as they grazed sidewise of the slope.

Tika Bhakta asked me, "Do you know how those paths were made?" Before I could make a mundane answer, he went on, "Those were made, and ones like them all over the world, when Hanuman's monkeys searched everywhere, back and forth, for Sita after the demon Ravanna stole her away from Prince Ram, her husband." I looked at the paths with new eyes. They, too, were connected to the sacred world that surrounded us every day in Nepal.

The trail wound between the foothills, climbing slowly till we saw a stele on top of a small bare peak. Bhuban sprang into the lead and presented the monument to us proudly. His grandfather, Jnan Kaji's fine old father, had erected it. It told the story that made the place famous. The King of Banepa's three sons had been roaming the hills one day when they came upon a starving tiger and her three cubs. All were near death,

On the trail to Nam Buddha. Syam is carrying a butterfly net.

thin and almost unable to move. The two elder sons went on, but the youngest stayed in pity, wondering how he could help her. He had no food to give the mother tiger, so he took his knife and cut a piece out of his own arm to feed her. She ate it, began to grow stronger and then sprang at the young prince and killed him. When his brothers came back to find him they saw only a pile of bones, a healthy mother tiger and three frolicking cubs. The story bothered me, but the boys all felt that it had been a noble act the prince had performed. "Would you rescue a tiger so she could eat you? Wasn't that a foolish thing to do?" I asked.

"I couldn't do it, but I do not have the noble soul the Prince had," said Bhuban. And the others all murmured assent. "*Ramro tio.*" (It was a noble, kind deed.)

On a crest a quarter of a mile above us was a white stupa shaped like an inverted bowl with a ceremonial finial on top. It was Nam Buddha, the Buddhist form, so different from the Hindu pagoda-shaped temples. We saluted it and I asked the boys if they had been north to the higher areas of Nepal, where everyone is Buddhist, where stupas, prayer flags, and water wheels abound. No they had not. "Why is it so different here?" I asked them. They didn't know, but it was one of the accommodations between the two religions that let them coexist so happily. "Here you grind grain with waterwheels," I said, "but there they are all for the gods. Some are twelve feet tall. They are all sizes. I wish you could have seen one I found. It was in a tiny stream below a waterfall. It was made of a turnip, with bits of wood stuck in for fins, and a small red rag at the top of its spindle which waved gaily as it turned saying prayers."

"Also I visited a monastery in the mountains with a reincarnated Rimpoche and many holy things."

"I will make a pilgrimage there," said Bhuban. "I, too," said the other Buddhists, Bikram and Raj Bhai. "We'll go too," said the Hindus, Lok Sudar, Tika, and Syam.

The land sloped and rolled away in all directions. To the

Monument erected by the grandfather of Bhuban (standing right) honoring the King's son who cut off a piece of his own flesh to feed a starving tiger and her cubs.

south the wooded mountains of the Mahabharat Lekh raised their heads to 9000 feet. Valleys and hills lay below us, rising in the north to the snow giants in their magnificent breathtaking line. We could see the peaks from Daulighiri in the west to beyond Everest and Makalu in the East. Several hundred miles of overwhelming beauty.

Bikram started to tear pages out of the Chinese magazine. We all sat down on the grass crosslegged and Raj Bhai took apart the separate bowls of the picnic kit. Everyone helped himself to curries and rice and radish pickles, and we all began to eat with our hands. The inexpert way I tossed food into my mouth was less embarrassing out here on the ground and I gazed around me trying to fix every fold and rise and pinnacle in my mind forever.

Nam Buddha Stupa on the sacred mountain where we picknicked. Left to right: Syam, Raj Bhai, the author, Tika Bhakta, Bhuban.

The feverish cold I had started with hadn't left me. The long walk back was exhausting. But I wouldn't have taken anything for that day.

It was times like this, when everything was glorious, that filled me with gladness and a great appreciation and love of Nepal. I knew my luck in being there. The beauty of the country, the frustrations of the school, the isolation of having no one of my own kind to talk to, the joy when some of my pupils really put ideas together, the wonderful festivals—it was all a whirling barrage of vivid impressions and emotions. Nothing was ever dull. Nothing was ever easy.

I can remember many days when things went wrong in the most exasperating and needless ways. I would start home discouraged and angry, but then, as I reached the bazaar, everyone—people I didn't know, as well as those I did—would smile at me so infectiously that I couldn't stay mad. Nepalis have the most beautiful smiles on earth.

It was those smiles and the glory of the mountains that pulled me through the hard times. Those and my curiosity to see what would happen next in this country, so wonderful, and so strange.

17

Ram Bhakta—The Rising Man

A SMALL CHILD had fallen asleep behind a basket of dried
corn cobs. He lay in shadow under the eaves in the
big kitchen which took up the whole of the fourth floor of the
house. The sound of voices half-waked him. His big dark eyes
batted open for a moment, then closed again. Drowsily he heard
his uncles talking.

"Now that Daju, elder brother, is dead, eh? And the
purification period is over."

"And Hari Devi, Daju's wife, is not well. She was never
strong." Kancha, youngest brother, drew sibilantly on his
cigarette through his cupped hand.

"She won't live long; that is sure," said the first voice.

"There is no one else, just the little boy. He doesn't know
what belonged to his father. We must take care of him." There
was a laugh.

The little boy, Ram Bhakta, lay still behind the basket. His
eyes were tight shut, but his heart had started to beat so hard he
thought it must be shaking him back and forth. The soft voices
were talking about him and his mother.

"This *pukkha* house, right here on the bazaar. We'll move
our store here. Maybe the boy will die, too."

"*Hola.*" (Very likely.)

"It won't matter. He can work in the store."

"And there are the rice fields. Good fields. We will manage
them, of course. For Hari Devi and the *bachcho*." Ram Bhakta,
the *bachcho* they were talking about, heard the younger uncle's
knee joint crack a little as he uncrossed his legs and got up off
the floor. Footsteps retreated, bare feet on mudded floor.

123

Ram Bhakta didn't move until long after they had gone away. At last he opened his eyes. A small, almost transparent lizard was climbing the wall. His eyes followed it without seeing. The boy was tiny, but he was six years old. That day was his sixth birthday. That morning he had sat only three feet from the basket he now lay behind, while his mother and uncles did him birthday homage.

His mother had gone to the temple early and come back with *prasad*, her own gifts blessed by the gods—rice and *tika* powder, fruit and vegetables, to use in the birthday *puja*. For a long time the ceremony had gone on. Offerings were placed before him and on his head and shoulders. His mother and uncles bowed to him. Each placed a red *tika* mark on his forehead. During all the two or three hours he listened gravely to the sacred words his mother recited. She was interrupted now and then by a fit of coughing, but she never seemed to forget a syllable. She knew when to pour water, when to wave the smoking lamp, when to throw rice. The immemorial ritual enveloped him. Constantly the three elders made signs of respect to him. He thought now of his uncles' dark faces smiling at him, and he knew fear.

But at the time he had felt only happiness and pride as they worshipped him like a god. They had eaten a feast of special foods, and afterward he and his mother had taken food down to the street and given it away in abundance to all who passed. Poor boys and girls held out their cupped hands. Women held out an end of their saris, even men were glad to take the *yomari* and the good cooked rice mixed with yoghurt, the fruit and vegetables. Little Ram Bhakta had stood proudly by, and watched the people being given the bounty of his birthday. Now he had heard his uncles plotting to take everything from him. He felt small and helpless. His mother sick? His home in danger? He was desperately afraid.

Ram Bhakta's face worked as he told me this story. Then he tossed his handsome head with its crest of black hair and smiled. "It is long ago," the 28-year-old Headmaster said, "But I never forgot. That day changed my life."

He was answering the question I had asked about how he got interested in education. "At first it was fear of my uncles," he said. "The happiest part of my day was the time I spent at my tutor's house at Wokutol beside the Ganesh temple. There were four of us. We would sit on the floor of his house or outside in the square. The shady side in summer, the sunny side in winter."

Their Nepali books were pages and pages of symbols, of the Devanagari script. In unison they chanted page after page. Sometimes the other boys were puzzled or their attention wandered. Always, it was Ram Bhakta's voice, high and clear, that led them unhesitatingly. I could imagine him, the gold circlet in his ear and his white teeth flashing. He loved school.

His mother insisted on sending him off each day to read. (The word for study and for read are the same in Nepali; so is the activity). The schooling was narrow, but Ram Bhakta absorbed all there was.

He went on to a bigger school, and the lessons got harder. It was the first real school in Banepa, with 20 boys coming almost every day. Here he found that he was the first boy in the class. It was easy for him to learn and remember. Surje Prasad, his best friend, son of the cloth merchant on my corner, would get him to help him with his lessons every day. It was part of the easy Nepali sharing of each other's lives, and Ram Bhakta delighted in being useful. Soon he was helping all the boys. When he was through teaching them, he couldn't forget the lesson if he tried. In school and study he was happy. When he was at home alone that old conversation of his uncles rang in his ears. He began to see education as a way to protect himself and his mother.

The uncles seemed kind and friendly now; they used the store on the ground floor of the house, but they paid rent for it. His mother managed the fields without their help. Her cough had disappeared. There seemed no danger of her dying. Still he felt driven. He must work to make a bulwark of education. He knew now that learning was his best chance.

The uncles asked Hari Devi, "Why do you bother to send him to school? It is a waste of time and money. He could be working in the store."

"I want him to learn."

"What for? We are doing well, and we can't read. Who needs to read?"

Ram Bhakta put in, "There is a questionnaire from the King. It asks can you read and write? Could your father read and write? Your mother?"

"A question from the King?"

"Yes, from His Majesty's Government. He wants to know who can read and write. Our teacher knows the man who was writing it down. He told us there are 132 men and 13 women, out of the 6,000 people in Banepa, who can write."

"See, people don't need it."

"It's the new thing to do. To be able to write down the words is good," said Hari Devi stubbornly. Ram Bhakta echoed her. He was 11 years old and still small. He had found a friend who encouraged him.

The *Pradhan Panch,* the headman of Banepa, who was beginning to take an interest in the bright-eyed young student, used his influence in helping to start a high school in Banepa the next year. It was just in time for Ram Bhakta to enter the beginning sixth class, which met in the Buddhist courtyard but in rainy weather retreated to the room where the red statue of Buddha rested between ceremonial appearances. Clustered at Buddha's feet, class members studied their lessons. From the beginning Ram Bhakta led his class.

After school the *Pradhan Panch* let the boy follow him around. "Run home and get my water pipe," he'd say, and Ram Bhakta would be off, bare feet flying over the uneven cobblestones. Or, "Here, Ram Bhakta, read me this paper." The *Pradhan Panch* was among the 132 men who claimed they could read and write, but he felt more confident if he heard the words read out loud to him.

The headman's power was growing. He frequently took the seven-hour walk into Kathmandu to find out what was going on in the capital. Sometimes he let Ram Bhakta go with him. It was a time of upheaval. For immemorial ages Nepal had been shut off from the world. Now its mountain-fastnesses had been breached; new influences were flowing in; tentatively Nepal was reaching out toward the wave of the future.

The *Pradhan Panch* wanted to catch the wave and ride it in. He wanted to take his town of Banepa with him. Most of Banepa did not want to be taken anywhere. Ram Bhakta, though, thrilled to the prospect. One day his mentor said to him, "Things are changing. You might change your caste name. Koke-Shrestha has a fine ring. I'll back you up." His mother shrank from so drastic a step, but was persuaded. She adored Ram Bahkta. If he and the *Pradhan Panch* thought it right, she would not object.

Much of Banepa was wary of any innovation. His uncles inevitably lined up with the conservative faction . They looked from the corner of their eyes at their nephew's position of favor with the progressive leader. They deplored his continuing to study at an age when he could have held a man's place in the store or the fields.

But his master told the boy, "All the *thulo manche haru* will be educated men. Study hard. There will be a place for you in the new Nepal."

His eighteenth year, the year he was a senior in high school, was a good year. He finished at the head of his class and passed the SLC in the first division. There was hope unlimited. He would be a *thulo manche* doing something important in Kathmandu. King Mahendra had proclaimed a new con-stitution, providing for voting for local *Panchayats*. No one had ever voted before. It was exciting. The people of Banepa gathered at Wokutol and voted the *Pradhan Panch* to the top spot he had held before. They elected four men under him, feeling a new importance in themselves.

A college was started in the capital and Ram Bhakta was a student there with the help of his patron. Again he did creditably and graduated high up in his class. He wore Western style pants and a shirt and leather shoes. He removed the small gold hoop from his ear. He looked at his uncles in their not-very-clean *dhotis* and bare feet. He wondered how he could ever have feared them. They gave him respectful treatment now, and he knew they bragged about their educated nephew.

At the end of fourteen years of schooling (the required number of years in Nepal for a B.A. degree) he graduated. The dream was unrolling itself on schedule. But a great blow fell. The *Pradhan Panch* was killed in a plane accident, and with him went Ram Bhakta's best chance of advancement in a land where everything depends on influence.

Nevertheless, he managed, with a government scholarship, to go to the new Tribhuvan University for an M.A. He was the only man in Banepa who had that much education and the town was proud of its smiling son.

The Managing Committee of the high school, which now met in its own new brick building instead of a temple yard, offered him the Headmastership. He accepted. At 23 he was younger than any of his teachers; and without his knowing it, a small cloud of discontent rose in the factions of Banepa.

By this time he had married, and had two little daughters and a baby son. His mother and uncles had chosen his wife, a girl of his own caste from a village six miles along the trail to Nam Buddha. Janaki Devi was pretty and slender. Dressed in scarlet and gold, she had been carried in a *dooli* to his house, a 14-year-old girl leaving all the people she knew and loved, to be the lowly daughter-in-law under Hari Devi.

She had sat silently with downcast eyes through the ceremonies of the wedding. Now, years later, she was still silent, though she raised her beautiful eyes from time to time.

Hari Devi was not unkind to her, but she was stern. Janaki Devi kept the house immaculate. Every morning she mudded the kitchen floor, and the doorway, and the little path that led around the corner of the house to the bazaar. No one ever came too early to find it freshly done. She cooked under Hari Devi's eye. She washed clothes by the public faucet with the other young wives. She helped to carry the wheat from the fields, to thresh it, and to take it to the mill. Hari Devi planted the flowers, conducted daily worship, and acted as hostess. Hari Devi was *thakali naki*, the senior woman whose ritual and social position was important. Both women vied to have everything perfect for Ram Bhakta when he came home from school or from gossiping in the bazaar.

The only time husband and wife were alone was at night when they crawled under the mosquito net over the pad in one corner of the living room. It was the only place where Ram Bhakta was free from the obligation to revere his mother first and always. It would have been wrong to speak tenderly to his wife in front of his mother, but when they were by themselves, tenderness and a tentative understanding began to develop.

The household continued the same as ever when Ram Bhakta was awarded a government fellowship and went off to the United States to study at the University of Wisconsin. Nepali wives are used to being outside the lives of their husbands. Janaki Devi waited quietly.

For the young man from Banepa, it was a glimpse into an unimaginable world, a marvelous but confusing world. In the end it was a paralyzing experience, but this he did not yet suspect.

18

Ram Bhakta's Falling Star

ON HIS WAY TO STUDY at the University of Wisconsin, Ram Bhakta stopped in California. Someone took him to South High School in the town of Torrance. They asked him to tell the students about his school in Nepal. Looking around at the bright building with all the trappings of modern American education, he told them of Ajad High School's mud floors, of its glassless windows, its lack of water, toilets, electricity, books and equipment. It had no science laboratory, or gym, or any of the shining equipment he saw here.

The earnest, personable, young headmaster with his flashing smile and his tales of his poor school in Nepal caught their imagination. They would help him. The school and the town worked for a year to put on a fair to raise money. It was a great success. They wrote Ram Bhakta they were putting $5,000 in a savings account for Banepa until he could make his plans. To Banepa it was a windfall of epic proportions.

Ram Bhakta's first reaction, after one wild surge of joy, seems to have been fear. Secretly he told the Chairman of the Managing Committee of the high school. They took the new *Pradhan Panch* into their confidence. For weeks they held private conferences. Hints began to leak out—intimations of great good fortune, but always with a scent of danger about it. Such a sum entrusted to them was frightening. It was unheard of. Would someone steal it? They used the word *khannu*; and, they kept asking, would someone eat it? Even though the money was in a safe account in the U.S., they were fearful, even while elated.

130

In Ram Bhakta's head danced visions of schools he had seen in America. At the bottom of his consciousness was the staggering gulf between those schools and Ajad, between them and the whole Nepali educational system. But here was a princely sum to spend. He visualized Ajad as a shining metal and glass construction.

The town leaders wanted an auditorium to meet in, instead of the dirt of Wokutol square. Ram Bhakta wanted a science laboratory like the wonderful ones he had seen. He wasn't stupid, so he had a great deal to hide from himself. Buried deep, was the knowledge that no such laboratory could be built in Banepa for fifty times the money. But it all seemed possible so long as the gift was a secret. At an early stage, Ram Bhakta had shared the problem with the Peace Corps hoping for guidance.

The most important men in town mulled it over together, making excited suggestions to each other, their ideas glowing brighter and brighter. But they drew back from "doing something." Any decision would be a mistake. Furthermore, to decide on one thing would be to rule out all the other beautiful possibilities that danced before them.

By the time I came to Banepa in February, 1969 the gift had been announced to the town, along with the decision, or half-decision, to build a science laboratory. They still thought maybe they could build an auditorium too. However, Ram Bhakta told me firmly that they would have the lab under roof by the time the monsoon rains came in June.

Time, which slides by gently and unnoticed in Nepal, did just that. No decision was made. A year later there was a new Regional Officer at the Peace Corps, a young man who had some architectural training. Americans love to make decisions and get things done. He took Ram Bhakta and me to look at two science labs in Kathmandu—one of them at a school run by Americans for the children of Americans stationed there. He drew up plans. He found a construction company. He got an estimate. It came to almost double the amount of money available. Then the enterprising young American vanished.

He was around Kathmandu for a few months longer, but Ram Bhakta could never find him. However, the Headmaster felt that a tremendous amount of action had already been taken. He had done all sorts of things toward a solution. Maybe someone else would come along and finish the job. More months went by, and nothing happened. I was keeping strictly out of it. The decision, I felt, must be a Nepali one, but finally I did ask Ram Bhakta, "Do you have confidence in the firm who drew up the blueprints and made the estimates on a new science lab?"

"Yes, they are very good."

"You could ask them just what they *could* build for the money you have."

"Well, maybe. The money is in the bank in America drawing interest. It is growing." With a gesture he sketched a pile. A pile growing sky-high.

I couldn't entirely suppress a sigh of exasperation. If Banepa was to make use of the generosity of Torrance, California, it was going to have to take action. It vacillated. What seemed wisdom and prudence to me, threatened some vague kind of disaster in the Nepali mind. There the matter rested, waiting for the fullness of time.

Other kinds of action Banepa understood. Intrigue and jockeying for power are things the East perfected when our ancestors wore bearskins. The gift had boosted Ram Bhakta's prestige. But time passed and the faction that had been against him began to mutter again. There was rivalry between the *tols* of the town, between families who had grievances against each other built up over generations. Now there was a new focus— the Communists. The little red plastic booklets *Thoughts of Chairman Mao*, which fit so neatly into the breast pocket of modern Western shirts, was a status symbol. Cadres from the nearby camp of Chinese road-builders visited Banepa. Ideas and rumors filtered into Banepa. Some of the people who had always been against the Headmaster wondered why Ram Bhakta had gone to imperialist America to study. Some held his change of name against him.

What they talked about, though, was high fees for tuition. The failing grade of the popular son of one of the town's richest men. The high cost of textbooks. Teachers who didn't meet their classes. These and a thousand and one other nits of discontent. It wasn't until the summer of 1970 that Ram Bhakta's opponents brought it to the test.

The day it began I had been in Kathmandu to cash my paycheck. (I never admitted in Banepa that I received the huge sum of $40 per month.) When I came home on Sunday afternoon, everyone clustered around me in the bazaar with the news. The students were striking. There had been a parade with placards—DOWN WITH RAM BHAKTA. FIX THE ROOF. LESS TUITION. Dilip, his eyes wide, told me, "The roof will fall down and kill someone." Prakash said, "Ram Bhakta is no good." "The teachers don't teach half the time," began Taro. But Ram Bhakta came brushing through a group of hill women with *dhokas* full of fresh *sal* leaves on their backs. My students fell silent as he went with me toward my house. He came in and talked for three hours.

It had begun, he said, with an ultimatum by the student leaders demanding his removal. They had taken it to the Managing Committee of the high school. The Committee supported him, and stood by him when he answered the strikers' nine demands in a public confrontation.

"I answered them all, except that they want to fire me. But some people say I'm a fine headmaster." He looked at me hopefully, his head on one side. His eyes were worried. "The school can't operate on lower fees. The sixth grade only pays 7 rupees a month (70 cents). They want not to have to pay for days they miss by starting school late. But if we let them do that, they will start even later and miss more school. They want the roof fixed, and of course, so do I. I told them I hope we will have money enough next year. They want the teachers to come to class on time and teach the whole period, and the teachers have promised to do it. They want free access to the science lab."

"That's a joke," I said. "That little storage closet is no laboratory. You know if we let them have free access every bit of equipment we have would be ruined in 15 minutes. You can't even put posters up anywhere at school because the students would tear them down. You have to protect even the class schedules under bars."

"I know, " he said sadly. "I told them so. They seemed to understand. They had no more to say. But they are striking. Of course it isn't just the students. There are forces behind them." When I asked what forces, he was vague.

The whole faculty went up to school every day as usual, but much more promptly. The strike was infinitely more interesting than teaching.

The paths to school from east and west Banepa join a couple of hundred feet short of the building, and pass between two little hills. The student leaders stood on the east hill, a sort of picket post. None of the girls came to school, but most of the boys came on up to see what was going on.

Ram Bhakta stood on the west hill, an encouragement to strike-breakers. A few boys went through the pass and on to school. Most gathered on the east knob around the strike leaders. These strikers were the officers of the tenth grade, except the president, my friend Tika Bhakta, who held aloof from the excited agitators with dignity.

Subhadra stood on top of his hill. Ram Bhakta told me, "Subhadra hates me because I exposed him in a flagrant case of cheating." I marvelled silently. It must have been flamingly flagrant indeed. "The boy is a bully," he added. "And a malcontent. He uses the tuition money his father gives him to buy sweetmeats at the tea shack at school. When that is gone he borrows from the little boys and never pays them back."

Headmaster Ram Bhakta and the author.

Though he was not in my tenth grade biology class I knew Subhadra as a tall shock-haired boy, prominent around school. A prominent cheater, too, at the time of my one and only invigilation. His lieutenant, Prem Lall, I didn't know much better. He took biology, but he was in class less than half the time. The two of them swaggered and laughed on their hill, the center of a group of smaller boys. Ram Bhakta held his ground alone on his hill. As I set foot on the arcade, the *piun* rang the hand bell, keeping up the pretense that school was in session. This admission that I was more apt to be on time than the tinny clock he sometimes forgot to wind was the *piun*'s daily compliment to me.

Seventh grade science was scheduled, but no one was in the room. After a glance I went to the office. A chess game was starting, which was to grow into a tournament. Everyone watched the play until Subhadra and Prem Lall appeared on the arcade at the end of the corridor to the office. We all went out behind Ram Bhakta.

Subhadra and his cohorts stood on the ground, a couple of feet below the arcaded porch. Prem Lall read out the demands again, with one addition. Why had the school closed for America's landing on the moon, and not for the Russian Sputnik flight? Ram Bhakta patiently explained the school's stand on each issue as he had done before, adding that news of Sputnik's flight had not been known in Banepa till some days later. I spoke up saying I wished I had been there so we could have talked in science class about how important it was.

Prem Lall amused me by saying I never brought the microscope to class. "Prem Lall," I laughed, "how would you know? You hardly ever come to class. You missed all the times we used it."

Ram Bhakta argued them down on every count and there was a confused motion toward the classrooms, but the strikers blockaded the doors and windows and kept the others out. The two soldiers sent up to protect the school stood woodenly watching.

Every day the teachers signed in and out. As time went on a few more boys came, and some of them went to the classrooms. Ram Bhakta had the teachers stay in their rooms more and more. One day I had five children in seventh grade, so I took them, as I often did with small groups, to the "laboratory." They were fascinated by the plastic man made to be put together organ by organ. The window filled with a watching group. After a while I let them come in and sent the first ones out.

When the bell rang I went back to the office, absentmindedly locking my umbrella inside. It was of the big, black, old-fashioned kind that everyone used. In monsoon season you needed it all the time, either for the frequent rain, or for the fierce sun that came out the moment the rain stopped.

A few minutes later Subhadra appeared at the office doorway, a self-satisfied smile breaking through his attempt at gravity. He looked at us teachers. "You are prisoners. You cannot leave the office. This is a lock-in." He used the English word, a cull from the Communist Chinese Magazine, which dwelt on American strikes.

Through the door at the end of the corridor I could see the soldiers lounging outside. They did not look like a source of help. I looked at Ram Bhakta. He did not seem excited. Neither did the others. It was 11 o'clock. They had nothing to do. They weren't going to resist.

"But our students are threatening us," I cried. They shrugged. Uninterested.

"If we want to walk out we can do it all together." No one moved. I talked to Ram Bhakta, Krishna Prasad, Jnan Kaji. They were all for doing nothing. I thought of all the hours ahead, and of myself, a lone female, in one bare room with all these men. I realized the male advantages they had. At a pinch a window would suffice for them, I thought. I misunderstood them, but I thoroughly understood my own problems. I was not going to stay all day with no ladies' room. I was curious to see what would develop, but not curious enough to put up with hours of boredom among these Newari-speaking men.

I would test the situation. I went out to the end of the corridor. My lab door was the next one along the arcade. "I just want to get my umbrella," I said. "No, No!" the kids shouted. "You are a prisoner. You are locked in." They crowded tight against the door, sealing it.

"Come back, Root! They'll beat you to dust," Gobinda shouted. I retreated.

"Come on, let's get out of here," I said. "I'm not going to let my students hold me prisoner. "Come on, Ram Bhakta!" He shook his head. I looked around. No one else wanted to leave. "It's better to do nothing," Ram Bhakta said.

The office corridor ran back from one end of the ell-shaped arcade. No one was behind the ell or outside the office windows at the moment. Across from me was a window looking out on the back of the ell. In a chair by the window sat the younger of the two *piuns*, the one whose mouth was perpetually open in surprise. I motioned to him to get up. The students looking down the corridor could see him, but not me. He stared at me, mouth still open, no comprehension in his eyes. I motioned again. This time he moved, but he took the chair with him. I needed it to stand on to reach the window sill. I was afraid the strikers would see what I was about.

Finally I persuaded him to put the chair back and leave it. Out of the corner of my eye I could see Ram Bhakta's disapproving look, but I quickly stepped on the chair, put a foot on the sill, and jumped, falling ungracefully to my knees. There was no one behind the building but me. I heard no cry, but I could have been seen if anyone were in any of the classrooms.

I scrambled to my feet and walked along the back of the ell, trying to combine dignity, unconcern, and speed. As I rounded the corner I saw that Ganesh Himal had emerged from the monsoon clouds and uplifted its shining triple peaks into a patch of clear blue. I felt it a good omen for my next test.

There were a hundred yards to go across the school grounds to get to the downward path. Eyes straight ahead, and heart racing, I marched across it. A boy started running after me, and I trembled, but when he came up to me it was Bikram of the English Conversation Club calling, "*Ratima tapaico gharma aune?*" I answered testily, "I'm pretty fed up with the students at the moment, but come to the club tonight if you wish."

Leaving Bikram to guard my rear, I went on down. Once again I'd been forced by my culture to action, where the Nepalis infinitely preferred inaction. Time stretched before them in unhurried sequence. No one but I felt it was a waste to spend it sitting in the office. No one else felt he had to assert himself. No one else worried about the problems ahead. In a land where boys went barebottomed until they were eight and men squatted to relieve themselves beside the road, I didn't suppose calls of nature would be a problem to my colleagues. I just didn't want to be there when they started urinating out the windows.

It turned out to be another instance when I had misjudged what would happen. Later, Gobinda showed me an account of the strike he had written in English. There were nice bits about the students threatening to beat us to dust, the soldiers standing like scarecrows in a field, the Peace Corps teacher's narrow escape through a window. Two hours later the men began to be troubled by the problem I had worried about.

Evidently teachers have too much dignity to use the simple public solution I had feared. The strikers wouldn't let them out to go to the latrine. They begged to be allowed to just go to an empty room. The rest of the story was a mixture of their distress and pious remarks about how the students were "killing their time instead of studying." Gobinda wrote, "Asa Kaji was in disaster." At about four the students drifted away and the teachers hurried out.

Next day Ram Bhakta was busy interviewing the Managing

Committee after deploying his teachers at the doors of their classrooms. Everyone was staying outside, saying, "It's easier to go to the latrine." Conversation is always quite open on the subject. Day by day more children came to class. Ram Bhakta had the teachers teach whoever came. Under his calm eye more and more boys came to school every day. At the end of a fortnight the strike quietly died. The girl students reappeared. School resumed its sluggish course. Ram Bhakta's patience had won. Nothing changed. Teachers still taught less than half a period.

Yet Ram Bhakta's plans went on burgeoning. He would come to my house and tell me the latest. It might be a dormitory, or it might be new shelves for the "library." Or a course on flower arranging or King Lear. These in a provincial town where the simplest modern English is hardly understood, and flowers are for the gods. On his next visit he was going to persuade His Majesty's Government to make Banepa a vocational school. It all mingled together in his mind in a bright Western light of never-never land. Of the one real possibility—the science laboratory for which he had $5,000 awaiting him in California, he spoke ever more vaguely.

Time passed. Soon it would be Thanksgiving in America. I arranged with the Deputy Chief of Mission in Kathmandu to get a can of cranberry sauce from the PX. Om Bahadur found me a specially good chicken. I made a pumpkin-like pie from squash. I invited Ram Bhakta and his wife and mother, Jnan Kaji and Krishna Prasad and their wives. I told them to come at 6:00. "Morning or evening?" they asked. Many of their *pujas* begin in the early hours. When they arrived Thanksgiving night, the men were alone. It was too great a deviation from custom to bring their womenfolk with them. However, we had a pleasant evening. and at one point Ram Bhakta said, "Next time we must bring our *satis* with us." He never did, though. Janaki Devi remained always in the background, and would as long as her mother-in-law lived. Ram Bhakta could not even bring himself to escort his mother to my house.

Once he said, his fine eyes wistful, "Yours is a really developed country." The label undeveloped, that we attach to half the world, rankled. He told me, "If someone would make a plan for us, we could use the parts we wanted. We don't know how to make a plan for curriculum and administration." The impossibility of a leap over several centuries of development in a decade paralyzed him.

I thought of the teachers who didn't come to class, who never made lesson plans, of the terrible textbooks, the children who wandered in late, if at all. I remembered those who failed math and English every year, only to be promoted to flounder at a higher level. And the community whose parents put schooling far down their list of priorities.

And I reminded myself once again that 20 years ago there was no school. They had made such a big leap into an unknown undertaking, guided only by the half-understood example of a foreign culture. No wonder it was all too much for Ram Bhakta.

He and I had talked of all those problems before. It was no use going into them again. I thought about the philosophy of learning. "To learn and be able to use what he or she has learned, a person must *understand*," I said earnestly. "There must be some sense to what he learns. If he can't fit the facts together, they are no use to him. It is like a puzzle. You fit one piece of knowledge to another until you have a picture you understand and remember. As you fit piece after piece together, the picture gets clearer."

"That's all right for you. We don't know enough to do it that way."

"But, Ram Bhakta, it's not how much you know. It's a way of looking at things. If a piece of the puzzle is separate it means nothing."

He shook his head.

I tried again. "It's not good enough to teach facts in a helter-skelter manner, to be spewed up again at exam time."

But I was speaking to an age-old tradition in which the word had mystic value. An honored and esteemed man might spend years repeating "*om mane padme hum*" or "*Hari Krishna, Hari Krishna*." Ram Bhakta was a Hindu, not a Buddhist; but the prayer flags and water wheels, that ceaselessly wafted holy words into the air, were not foreign to him. Words were magical. What difference in what order they were learned?

Ram Bhakta waved my ideas aside. "What I really wanted to tell you," he smiled, "was about the College they are starting in Banepa. We have 20 students already. They want me to be Vice-President. They call it Kavre College. It will meet in the high school building in late afternoon until money can be raised for a building of its own."

I was speechless. Finally I managed a weak, "Sounds fine." Then, "And the science building with the money waiting for you in California?"

"Oh, yes, we'll have that, too. Banepa will be a great town."

Gradually his smile faded. "But how? I'm stuck here with my Headmastership. They are supposed to pay me 250 rupees a month ($25) but they don't always do it. When I go to Kathmandu to look for a job, all I can find is tutoring. And I have an M.A. What can our students really hope to do?"

We sipped the glasses of spiced Nepali tea my cook brought us. We turned to stare out the window at the courtyard and the women looking for lice in each other's hair. The children playing in the dust.

"And most of them think they are going to be doctors," I said, referring to an attitude study I had made.

"What is the answer? In the beginning I thought education would make me a *thulo manche*. You still need important connections or you can do nothing. I overcame my uncles who would have taken my property. I haven't feared them for a long time. But everything is changing too fast. I'd rather have my uncles for an enemy than this vague new kind of life I can't understand. And I have been to America." Then he pulled himself up proudly and smiled at me. "All I can do is wait."

In the end he waited too long. One day in 1972 a letter came from Torrance, California. It was four years since the money had been given to Banepa. As no one had ever found a use for it, it was being given to a school in South America.

It had been pie in the sky and the Nepalis had never been able to persuade themselves to eat it. Or even to believe it was quite real. It was a mirage, and it vanished as mirages must.

With the loss, Ram Bhakta's prestige fell. The next summer there was another strike and this time they drove him out. Some believed, he had "eaten" the money. When I last saw him he was disconsolate. The store and his fields gave his family a living. The bright dreams had gone. The whirlpool of a world changing too fast had sucked him down more surely than his uncles' greed could have.

19

Krishna Prasad

KRISHNA PRASAD is a poet, and, as a poet must be, he is a man whose inner voice sometimes drowns out the common chorus. His poems are for children and concern everyday things, but he is unconventional and his life does not fit the bred-in-the-bone pattern of Banepa.

He broke inflexible rules of the society in which he lives by marrying a woman of a caste lower than his own. For this he will pay the penalty all his life, and so will his children. He gave up the usual secure caste and family life for Uma. Yet he is not unconventional enough to stroll through the streets by her side.

Walking casually through the streets together would be unthinkable. It is only on a pilgrimage to a temple or to a family gathering that a husband and wife of Banepa go out together, and then she walks behind. That Krishna Prasad and Uma should have gotten acquainted at all was a severe lapse of decorum. Brides and grooms usually do not meet each other until the wedding ceremony begins. Ram Bhakta told me he had insisted on being allowed to see his wife from a distance before he would agree to marry her, but that was an unusual modern idea. Krishna Prasad had eloped.

He did walk and talk with me, and this was another sign of his social daring. I, of course, was outside all rules. He often visited me, often invited me to come to visit him. To reach his door I walked past the sunken shrine where a stone Buddha sat on a carven lotus. I passed a well, unused now that water was piped down from the hills to the public faucet. No one drew water from this well, but once a year the neighborhood gathered to clean it on the day when all the snake gods were safely absent because that was the day snakes all went home to their family shrines to worship their own family gods, their *kul devotaharu*.

We mortals pasted bright colored pictures of the snake gods beside our doors on that day.

With hardly a glance at the mossy well, I continued on to Krishna Prasad's. I went through a passageway under one house, and another under Krishna Prasad's own dwelling. On the other side was the upper brick pool at Wokutol with its stone statues. I stopped beside Krishna Prasad's heavy wooden door, which stood open.

A Nepali would have walked in, but I stood outside the door saying his name until Krishna Prasad poked his head out a window and invited me to come up. I climbed the first flight of stairs and left my shoes on the landing, stepping into the small room where I knew he would receive me. He would be sitting on a pallet at the far end of the room. I would join him there. It was, I knew, the family bed at night.

We talked about many things. Sometimes his three black-eyed children tumbled over him while he talked. Uma never joined us. Like Krishna Prasad, she taught school. Hers was an elementary school. After school she was always busy working in the kitchen.

Krishna Prasad had never gone to school himself. His family had hired a tutor for him, but he never managed to pass the SLC exam. Nevertheless, he had tutored a few young children, sometimes in his family's house but usually in the sun outside, or in an empty cubicle in the neighboring brass-seller's house, depending on the weather.

One sunny day the children were droning their syllabary in chorus and he was lolling back listening idly to the rhythm, not thinking at all. In his mind words began to form:

> As they're chanting, learning enters.
> Learning enters their young minds.
> Saraswati, God of learning
> Opens up their childish minds.

He was excited. He repeated it softly to himself, changing the last line to "Gives to children wisdom's boon."

He held up a finger. "*Ramro sanga sunna na!* (listen well!)," he said, and sang out his little verse, accenting the rhythm. The children broke into delighted smiles.

He gave me a couple of his books and he read aloud to me. He told me about the day he had begun to hear poems in his head. He was 18 years old. At that moment when his first poem came to him, he caught sight of a girl in a red-bordered black sari, the sari worn by the Jyapu caste of peasants.

"Go on with your reading," he had told his class. He must have eye and mind free to follow the lilt of her walk, as her bare feet stepped delicately among the uneven stones. She turned to speak to a friend, and he saw she was the daughter of the small farmer who owned a couple of fields up by the Bhimsen temple. How bright her eye was and how sweet her smile.

"So," said Krishna Prasad to me, twelve years and three children later, "that day I began to write poetry and to love my wife. All in the space of five minutes."

He shifted his position slightly and looked into my face as he told his story. Of course he knew she was not a suitable wife for him. Her caste was too low; and caste, decreed by god and religion, is the essence of the person.

In the most ancient Rig Vedic times the Hymn of the Primeval Man sings that Brahmans and Chetris were created from the mouth and arms of the cosmic sacrifice, the peasants and merchants from his legs, and the artisans from his feet. As a low caste Jyapu, Uma was completely unacceptable to his family. They could not, by Hindu rule, eat food or drink water that she had touched. Or eat in company with her. How could she fill the role of daughter-in-law, which was to work and cook for the family?

"I knew all that," said Krishna Prasad, "but I paid no attention. I thought only of that girl. It took six months before I could have courage to speak to her. One day we passed in the street. I remember it was summer and she had some yellow guavas in her hands. I put my hands together and said

'*Namaste.*' She dropped her eyes, but I could see her lips curve in a lovely smile. After that everything seemed simple and inevitable."

He looked out the window at the pool and its statue of Ganesh, built beside one of the ancient city gates. Long before that gate and the vanished city walls were built, caste ruled the lives of everyone here.

"After about a year we understood each other without having had more than a half dozen momentary meetings, or any real chance to talk to each other. There is no place to meet privately in Banepa. Everywhere there are people." He sighed.

"We met one night, and ran away together. I brought her home to my family next day. No one wanted to speak to us. The room my parents grudgingly gave us (which later would be for our children too) was the smallest and worst room in the house. Never mind, it was ours. It was the only place where we could whisper to each other. At night we would sit on our pallet, which took up half the room, and hold each other tight."

He smiled at memories not to be shared. "It may be different in America, but in Nepal a son does not talk with his wife in the presence of his mother and father." I nodded. This I had heard over and over. "Besides, my parents were angry. My wife couldn't come into the kitchen, where the family shrine and daily worship is. She had to eat all alone in another room. They kept reminding us that her touch was pollution to them. 'I am very kind to let you into the house above the ground floor' my mother told my poor wife.

"At night she would weep in my arms and I would try to comfort her. Night after night. One I remember especially. She was tired. Too tired to . . ." He looked away and paused. She said to me, "Your mother has kept me working every moment today, from 4:30 this morning when you all got up to worship. She won't let me make offerings to your gods. She gives me all the worst jobs. I carried 25 big jars of water from the faucet at Tin Dada. And how much else beside! She doesn't even look at me. She just snaps out an order."

"I'd been trying all the time to tell my wife things would get better, but this time I said, 'Go home and visit your parents for a while.' What a smile came on her face, but then she was sad again. 'But I'll miss you. Even if it is so hard here, I'll miss you. Oh, I'll miss you!'

"But I wanted her to go home and be the pampered daughter for a while as all girls are in their own families. In her own home every girl-child is a goddess. It is always hard for a bride to go to a new family. That's why you see brides sitting in their decorated sedan chairs, in their new red saris and gold jewelry, weeping. Even without all the extra trials I had brought on my poor wife it is hard. I felt sad that I had never thought beforehand how hard it would be for her.

"In a month she came back rosy and hopeful. We kept trying to withstand the slights of my family. We were more together in this than most young couples because we knew and chose each other ourselves."

He gave me a clear look. I could see pride in it. Even while he talked of their humiliations, he took pride in their independent choice. He lit a cigarette and began to draw on it through his closed fist without touching it to his lips. He resumed. "When our first child was born a son we thought things would be better, but it was only worse. My parents didn't recognize him or the little girl who came next. My mother and father said they didn't belong to them at all. They would give me no money to move away, but finally we found this cheap house. I'd been teaching my wife to read and write Newari, which is what she speaks, of course. She was able to get a job teaching second grade at the little village school outside the walled compound of the missionary hospital. You know our children are taught through the third grade in Newari only, since it is the language they speak at home. After that they start to learn Nepali. Her school is in the little village where she grew up, and the littlest girl stays with my wife's mother in the daytime. My wife goes to their house every morning for morning worship and breakfast.

I go to my family's house. We are divided. My family will never accept my children or my wife." He sighed deeply.

Just then the wife came into the room. Earlier I had seen her give the eldest daughter, Jethi, a *suka* and send her out to the bazaar. Now she carried a little white enameled dish with a fried egg and some *chura* on it. I was glad for the flattened rice to help me scoop up the soft egg. I gave her my best *namaste* and a smile in place of the thanks Nepalis never utter, and told her honestly that it was delicious.

One day Krishna Prasad invited me to come to dinner. He took me into the kitchen, the only one in Banepa I was ever invited to enter except Ram Bhakta's. We sat on little flat boards and, as always, they gave me more rice than I could eat, a good curry and pickles. I knew I was specially honored to be allowed in the kitchen, though this one could never quite be the center of the home it would have been had they been of equal caste.

Much later I heard that Krishna Prasad had been made Headmaster of a smaller high school at Nala. By that time his son was studying in Kathmandu. He had persevered in his struggle against the strictures of his Hindu caste, and was doing moderately well. His free mind had sustained him and opened a way to survive on his own terms.

20

A Mountain Village Named Wopi

FROM YEGYA'S HOUSE the world rolls away at your feet. His is the highest house in Wopi, and Wopi is the highest village above Banepa. Beyond it the terraces stop and the trail goes on a quarter mile farther to the top of the mountain. Long before I got to the house I heard the call, going on before me, "*Ayio.*" (She has come.)

As I arrived, Yegya was on the porch spreading a folded blanket on a mat for me to sit on with the gesture of a courtier offering a throne to his queen. He was of the caste to be a courtier, the Chetri or warrior caste, one of the twice-born who wear the sacred thread, next to the Brahmans in high rank. His ancestors were the conquerors who had come with Prithivi Narayan Shah to subjugate Nepal. True to their hill country origin and fierce independence, they had settled in widely spaced homesteads in the hills.

Yegya had just put down the little sickle with which he'd been cutting rice when he heard the call. His mother picked it up and went to help in the paddy. But first a little neighbor boy from some house out of sight had to come and take her place at the foot treadle where she and the sister-in-law had been hulling rice. Three little nieces were playing in the rice straw.

Every time I have been here Yegya's father, Beni Bahadur Thapa, he of the deep-set eyes, the black stubble beard, and the slow speech, has invited me to stay overnight. This time I've brought my sleeping bag.

150

First I must sit on the blanket for a few minutes. The house of Yegya's *daju*, elder brother, makes an ell with the main house. There is a stable on the right, a sign of wealth. Most hill families would be sharing the first floor with the cow and water buffalo. Also showing prosperity is the tin roof of the main house, the only roof in Wopi that isn't thatch. In the dooryard between these buildings the year's harvest of corn hangs from a pole, looking like a topiary tree of unhusked corn. It hangs high to avoid rats. The ears point down to shed the rain.

Wopi village home of Janak, shown with his mother and sisters. Lush growth provides practically all their food. Stored corn looks like a topiary tree.

On the downhill side of the house are banana and poinsettia trees, guavas, and a garden for soy beans, horse beans, onions, tomatoes, and squash—all the food that the family needs to supplement the corn raised on the high terrace and the rice from paddies carved out beside the mountain stream. Beyond the garden the land falls away to the wide-spreading view.

I had visited here several times since the beginning day of school when Yegya and his cousin Janak were the first children to arrive and break my solitary wait, but I had never been inside the house. Yegya had always entertained me on the porch. Now he took me in. This Chetri house is very different in plan from the tall Newar houses of Banepa.

The ground floor is one room, maybe 12 feet by 18, with stairs going up the middle. One side is the kitchen. The second floor is divided into two rooms, the smaller Yegya's. It is furnished with a raised bed (I never saw one in a Newar house) and a trunkful of books. Just under the low ceiling are hung pictures of the gods and a snapshot of Yegya's family taken five years ago. Beside that I jumped to see a photograph of two white-clad American Naval officers. After Christmas I had given my Christmas cards to my students, and Yegya had chosen one of an Admiral friend whose card that year had been a picture of himself and his son newly graduated from the Naval Academy. I wondered what Dave Ruble would think if he ever trekked in Nepal and wandered into this mountain house.

Yegya took me to the top floor under the roof and laid a staw mat along one wall for me. He spread the blanket for me to sit on and ran down to bring up pictures of Laxmi and Shiva to hang over my bed, for it was here I would sleep. He hung a wreath over the goddess' picture, put a red, white, and gold picture of Queen Ratna beside her and the snapshot of his family. Under these I sat in state.

"I have an egg I have been keeping in my room for you," he said and disappeared. I looked around. At the back under the

Cluster of houses sits among terraced fields in the scattered hill village of Wopi.

eaves were big baskets and jars of grain and one small basket of charred corn cobs for fuel.

Yegya came running up the stairs with a fried egg and some fresh hot *chapattis* on a bronze plate. He brought fresh water from their spring a quarter of a mile away, with apologies because neither the cow nor the water buffalo was giving milk just then. With my right hand I tore the *chapatti* and scooped up the egg, telling Yegya how good it tasted.

A lovely childish face peered from the stairwell. It was Thuli Miya, the eldest niece. On her shoulder hung the cross face of the baby on her back. Thuli Miya was only four and smaller than most American three-year-olds. Her black hair was square-cut across her forehead; her black eyes were enormous and black-lashed; her face was molded in beauty. I caught my breath.

She would grow into the kind of loveliness that in the old days, not far gone, might have caught the eye of a ruling Rana and raised herself and her family to heights of wealth and influence. But the King rules these days instead of the Ranas. He is a sober monogamist, and the path of a lovely hill girl is not apt to be so easy.

All three little girls came up when Yegya gave them permission. They sat in a row facing me, Thuli Miya, Sani Miya, and Kanchi, the baby. Each had an amulet around her neck. "Are the amulets made by the *Damai*?" I asked, meaning the Shaman. Yegya hesitated a moment and then said "Yes." Next morning I found out I had said it wrong. Again I'd confused aspirated and unaspirated words. Janak wrote it out for me in English. THE MAN WHO MADE THE *JANTAR* IS THE *DHAMAI*. THE MAN WHO MAKES THE TROUSERS IS THE *DAMAI*. That is a mistake I mustn't make. A *damai* is of very low caste, but a *dhamai* is highly respected.

The baby had been fussing and pulling at Thuli Miya's hair. She began to cry, but her face cleared and her mouth opened in a surprised O when I pulled a top out of my *jhola* and spun it. They gathered closer and I handed it to Thuli, but she couldn't make it go.

Janak and Raja Ram, another Wopi boy and one of my sixth graders, came in. We sat and spun the top. Thuli tried again and again and finally got it to wobble a turn or two. Janak slipped one of the six minute red glass bangles from Thuli's wrist and tossed it onto the spindle of the spinning top. It developed into a game that we played with variations with all six bangles until it was too dark to see. Janak always won.

The father, Beni Bahadur, returned from the fields. Carrying a tiny kerosene lamp, he came up to join us. I saw the lamp was made from a pill bottle I'd given Yegya the day before. In Banepa there is no trash. Purchases are wrapped in leaves. If you need a container you take it with you to the shop.

By the light of the little pill bottle lamp Beni Bahadur showed me his swollen foot. He had fallen from a terrace and a big stone, falling with him, had landed on his foot. That was two weeks earlier, but he still couldn't walk straight on it. He thought I might have medicine for it, but I had nothing that could help. Had he gone to the Adventist Hospital on the road to Chandeshwari? No, the fee (a few pennies) was too expensive.

The mother brought me *bhat* and *tarkari* on the bronze plate and the family took turns sitting with me while the others went down to eat in the kitchen, the sacred place where only caste members might eat.

After dinner the mother came and sat cross-legged with the rest of us to smoke a cigarette. Daju, Yegya's big brother, lit one also. He didn't look like the brother of small slight Yegya, whose face had no claim to charm until it curved into his shy smile. Daju was a big handsome man, a sergeant in the Royal Nepal Army stationed in Kathmandu. He talked about his job training new recruits. They were boys from all the hill towns of Nepal and he was their first teacher after they left their homes.

"I mustn't rush them too much, but I have to be firm. Everything is strange to them. They are amazed by the Kathmandu bazaars and crowds. By the temples and palaces. Most of them have never seen a rickshaw before, let alone a car. Yesterday a new man asked me whether a truck could jump sidewise and pounce on him. But they make good soldiers; they learn fast."

"You must be a good teacher," I said, and he answered, "*Ek dem ramro!*" (First rate!)

Without any schooling he would never make much more than his salary of 75 rupees a month ($7.50). That was not the point. He was a proud man, doing a necessary and important job well, and enjoying it. Janak said he too wanted to be a soldier. If he passed his SLC he could be an officer. Yegya wanted to work in a bank.

There was always the land, but when Yegya and Janak were sent to school (the first Wopi boys ever to go) it was decided that they wouldn't stay on the farm as their fathers had. They would try for jobs in Kathmandu.

Without influence one could get nowhere, but the family had a friend in the National Rastria Bank, on whom they counted. Nepal was changing; education might open doors. But only if one stood in well with the doorkeeper. In India, which is always in advance of Nepal in modernization (for good or evil), there was a host of unemployed, dissatisfied young people, educated and unable to find jobs to use their education and unwilling to take the jobs they could get. In Nepal the same problem was beginning.

If the job in Kathmandu doesn't work out, there is the land to come back to. Beni Bahadur said to me, "Even the most mighty Chetris can fall from power. Then they come back to a farm like this. All of us Chetris are equal. We haven't split up into a lot of sub-castes over the centuries, each trying to outdo the others."

Now Daju said, "Yegya's wife is coming here to live next month."

Surprised, I said, "Yegya, are you married?" Though I knew he was 17, the thin small boy looked about 10 to American eyes. His face broke into a smile as he admitted he'd been married almost a year.

"Where is she?"

"Over in Panchkal valley, in her father's house in Chautara. She has lived there until now."

"She's a Chetri of course."

"Of course. She's the sister of Daju's wife.

The mother said, "We need her help in the fields. She'll be a good worker like her Didi."

"Yegya, do you see her often?"

"Every once in a while."

"Will you be happy to have her come here to live?"

"Yes, very happy." This time the shy smile was shyer than ever.

I knew better than to ask what her name was. Husbands neither know, nor need to know, their wives' names. Once I'd asked my friend Krishna Prasad, "But what do you call your wife?" First he said, "I don't call her." Then he added, "I call, Eh!" Position in the family is enough name for most occasions. Amah, mother. Babu, father. Daju, elder brother. Didi, elder sister. Bahini, younger sister. Mama, mother's brother. Kaka, father's brother. Whatever the relationship, there's a name for it.

I knew Yegya and his bride would share his tiny room. She would be respectful and modest and hard working. Her sister, who had been the lowest person in the household, would shift some jobs to her Bahini. Except in their tiny room the bride and groom would pretend to pay little attention to each other. To talk together in front of the others would be a breach of manners. This subdued serious life would end a carefree, laughing girlhood. Married life begins in jolting earnest in her husband's home.

Yegya's bride was coming among kind people and would have her Didi for company. Still . . . . The father looked down at his swollen foot. "We'll be glad of her help."

Daju said, "She's small, only 14."

Daju's wife, the sister of the bride, didn't come into the room. She stood on the stairs and took the baby from Thuli's back. The baby was almost asleep; she gave a little whimper. It was Thuli who cried at losing her burden.

Flares flickered in the pill bottle lamp and in a tiny clay one. I heard a series of soft high notes.

"What birds would be singing this time of night?"

"Birds?"

"Don't you hear the singing?"

"Oh," Beni Bahadur looked at me in surprise. "*Musa ho.*"

I'd never heard mice or rats—the word means either—sing before, and I didn't quite like sleeping on the floor with them so near, sang they ever so sweetly. I was glad when Yegya brought a blanket and prepared to sleep beside me, though it was an attention I hadn't expected. He put mats in the windows to keep out the cold and whatever else might want to come in. He brought a brass pot (which I immediately decided never to use) and said it was *pisab garne taun* (literally: urine-doing place), a bit like the chamber pots our grandfathers took for granted. Then he blew out the light.

I had crawled into my sleeping bag and under cover changed into pyjamas. In the down bag I was warm and comfortable. I felt guiltily luxurious as Yegya shivered under his one cheap blanket. The *musa haru* rustled and sang, but I slept.

When it began to get light Yegya took down the mats from the windows. Inside my bag I dressed while I talked to the little girls who had crept back up the stairs. Yegya and I had planned for months that I would watch sunrise over the Himalayas from his mountain top. So, asking for five minutes lead time to look for a suitable bush, I started up the mountain. I passed two little girls going out to pick flowers for *malas* for the gods. Terror-struck by my white face, they broke into screams, and scampered away home to tell of the *bhut,* ghost spirit, they had seen.

Yegya caught up with me and we followed the upward path. The eastern sky was pink and rose. We walked faster than I comfortably could to get to the top before the sun did. We were close to 5,000 feet above sea level. There were no trees. They had all been chopped down for firewood long ago, and the bare round summit had been accented by a trench cut around it. It stood up like a nipple on a breast. We climbed onto the nipple.

It had been set apart this way, Yegya said, by the hill people who used to expose their dead here as the Tibetans do. Now that practice has stopped. Only the *dhamai* with their magical powers are buried on these high places.

We looked east. Against the darkly flaming sky the outlines of the *himals* showed black and jagged. One of them, not the highest from this vantage point, was *Sagarmatha,* Mount Everest.

We sat and watched the earth turn toward the sun. The mountains in progression from east to west changed from black to cold blue-white. To pale pink, then rose, gold, and pale yellow before they gleamed white and sparkling in the fully risen sun.

"There is an old story," Yegya said, "that the Mountains once were able to fly. They are gods, of course. But they used to have wings and sometimes flew from place to place. They were naughty and offended Brahma, so he cut off their wings and now they have to stay still. Their wings turned into clouds and hover always near them."

"What a lovely story," I said, but I looked at the solid-based northern wall of the world and wondered how anyone could imagine those mighty monsters flying. One day I would find out.

At last I looked away from the mountains and surveyed the world at my feet. Yegya and I traced together the trails we knew. He showed me the tract from Wopi to Nagarkot, where Shiva's sacred pool lies almost on top of the mountain. All the people of the hills converge there for the great annual festival where all the *dhamai* come, each with his own drummer and perhaps a few attendants. I had seen several *dhamai* dancing through Banepa in their white robes and peacock-feather headdresses, and I had followed after, accompanied by Jon, my Peace Corps friend from Dhulikhel. The *dhamai* danced the five-hour climb to Nagarkot. And, all night long the trails filled with pilgrims coming to camp, to enjoy the fair that accompanies such a gathering, to bathe in the sacred pool, and to see the magic dance that each *dhamai* performs.

We traced the trail to Nam Buddha, where Bhuban, Tika Bhakta, Raj Bhai and the rest had taken me. We swiveled toward Kathmandu, just visible over the saddle to the west. We could see the ancient and very sacred white stupa of Swayambhunath on its hill, and on this side of the city the great stupa of Bodhnath. Closer, we saw the golden spires and clustered houses of Banepa and Chandeshwari and a slice of our valley visible through a V between two slopes, one set with forest, the other terraced to the top. The picture was full of tiny detail. A toy bus inched up the long hill to Dhulikhel. Red and black dots on the trails were men and women with *dhokas* on their backs.

I thought of how I had first become interested in Wopi. Janak and Yegya had always worked hard in school and sometimes could take time afterward to come by my house when there was no work in the fields at home. They and Labakus, another good student, all came from the tiny village of Wopi. They held the same high standing this year in ninth class that they had last year in eighth. But where was Wopi? Janak had told me it was on a certain trail—the trail that a few years ago had been the beginning of the trail to Mt. Everest. Banepa had been the first night's camp in the early days of Everest Expeditions.

"But Yegya," I said, "I don't remember any village on that trail."

"Well, only the tea house and the primary school are really on the trail. There are about a hundred houses, but each one is in the middle of its own fields. The village covers quite a few miles, up nearly to the top of the mountain. Mine and Janak's are the two highest houses."

Janak spoke up, "Come up with us sometime to see. Dan Sir used to come up to visit."

I had heard of Dan Edwards. He was a Peace Corps Volunteer who had taught English in Banepa two years before. Janak told me Dan Sir had paid most of his tuition that year. It soon became apparent to me that as Dan had been Janak's friend, I was to be Yegya's, but it was Janak who had the courage to ask me. Or perhaps after Janak began talking to me Yegya's family decided it was only fair that I should be their special friend. The first time the boys took me up it had rained and the steep side-trail was slippery. I would never have made it by myself but the boys' bare feet were sure and steady. It took

me an hour and a half. Yegya and Janak said they made it every
day in 45 minutes.

That first day Yegya ran into the house to get a mat and
blanket for me to sit on on the porch. We looked at the
wonderful view and talked and I felt a kind of peace seep
into me.

It was the time I had to go away for a liver biopsy after
hepatitis that the boys really impressed me. There is no system
of substitute teachers, so no one would teach my classes while I
was gone. To satisfy my own conscience I gave them work to do
till I got back. But I had already fought and lost the battle of
homework. Since I was the only teacher who ever assigned any,
the children regarded it as an amusing eccentricity of mine and
just didn't do it. So I expected that nothing would come of my
careful instructions.

We had been studying the orders of plants as required for the
SLC exam. I'd taught them how to press specimens and had
brought many to class for them to draw. Now I asked them to
collect their own specimens of Cryptogams, press and label
them in their notebooks with proper classification, i.e.,
Cryptogam, Pteridophyta, fern; or Cryptogam, Thallophyta,
algae. I didn't really expect that they would do it.

When I returned I asked for their notebooks as a matter of
form. Janak, Yegya, and Labakus brought them forward. (And
those three only.) They were neat. They were correct. They
were complete. Even horsetails, which I had never been able to
find to show the class, were in their places, identified from the
pictures we had studied. I tried to act as though I'd expected the
work, and where was that of the other students? No wonder
those three stood first, second, and third in a class of 65. To cap
the record, the first boy in tenth class was from Wopi. Only
eight children, all boys, came to the high school from that
village. How could they hold four of the highest places? What
was their secret? If I could find their motivation, perhaps I
could impart it to others. I'd revolutionize the educational
system of Nepal.

I didn't, in spite of a survey study I made of the Ajad and other high schools for His Majesty's Government, pin down any important secret, nor did I revolutionize Nepal, but in the process of trying, I came to know Wopi.

"There is Janak's mother getting straw for a fire," said Yegya, bringing me back to the present. The sunrise had completed its gorgeous daily miracle. Reluctantly we stood up, hating to go. The sun was beginning to warm the earth. I took off my down jacket. We stopped at a spring, washed our hands and faces in the icy water, and brushed our teeth. I felt wonderful.

Janak was at the house when we got there. He took me to his home on a terrace 300 feet below to meet his mother. His father had already gone to his fields. The mother waited to meet me, surrounded by Janak's four little sisters. It is all right to ask a sister's name, but I still didn't learn their real names. They were Jethi, Maili, Saili, and Kanchi. That is, eldest daughter, second, third, and youngest. Janak asked if Yegya had given me milk and *dahi* (yoghurt), well knowing that both the cow and water buffalo of Yegya's father were dry. Proudly he brought a bronze bowl of milk, and a lovely fluted bowl of *dahi* and crisp, freshly made *chapattis* to the mat he had spread for me on the porch. Newar houses have no porches. Perhaps that was one reason I enjoyed so much the open porches of Wopi. In Banepa people gather and sit in the street in front of the house walls.

In a small flat place on the terrace was a *ping*, a sort of wooden ferris wheel, set up only at Dasain, the great Harvest Festival just past. They all took turns on it and Raja Ram and I rode it together. Then back to Yegya's, where I must eat again.

This time they took me into the sacred kitchen. I don't know how they justified it to themselves, or what purifying rituals they had to go through afterward. It would have been impolite to ask, and very likely, courtesy would have required an untrue answer. I always wonder at the precise information anthropologists collect. There are so many factors that can keep an informant's answer from being "true."

The kitchen was immaculate. I had noticed when I went out in the early morning that the doorway was already freshly mudded. So was the whole kitchen. By the small clay stove in the corner hung a clay lamp, almost exactly like those used in ancient Greece. To myself I counted the entire equipment. A heavy iron three-legged pot, a flat round iron for *chapattis,* the ball-shaped aluminum pot for cooking rice, a spoon, the bronze bowl and plate, two aluminum cups, and a standing cutter for slicing and peeling vegetables. It had a base in the form of a heron on which you put your foot to steady it. Of course all work was done sitting on the floor. Along the wall by the fire was something I had never seen before, a raised clay seat. Here they placed a mat for me to sit and eat crisp fried cakes and vegetables the mother cooked over a fire of weed stalks.

When I said I must go home they urged me to stay, and indeed I hated to leave. I stopped to drink of their spring and to sit on the col, looking at the sculptured terraces lapping at the hills—no, spurting in waves from the hilltops? I despair of painting the beauty of this land in words. The houses are as lovely as the terraces. Janak feels apologetic about his straw roof. I don't want to hurt Yegya, so I don't say how much superior the thatch is in beauty and insulation over the expensive tin.

There is quite a bit of rivalry between the two. I think they have their own spheres clearly marked out. Janak is the brightest and the elder. He is top dog and Yegya must never beat him. But Janak helps Yegya to be second. No one must challenge that either. My first invitation to Wopi was to Janak's house, but they took me to Yegya's instead. Janak once invited me to stay overnight at his house, but the day I was to go he came down to Banepa to tell me not to come. Since then I had always been at Yegya's. I had never seen Janak's house till now. Janak had an American friend in Dan. Now it was Yegya's turn.

What will become of these two bright boys? They had made

the brave attempt to step out of the past, which still holds their country fast, into an unknown future. In Wopi the age-long patterns of life show no sign of breaking up around them. The security of the past is still theirs to claim. They hold onto that while trying themselves in the changing world to be entered by education.

21

Someone Who Speaks My Language

ONE NIGHT as I ate dinner I was practicing throwing food into my mouth. With my right hand of course; the left hand is polluted even though Nepalis always wash their hands before a meal. Nepalis toss food into their mouths neatly and politely. As for me, I either hit myself in the face or splatter it all around me. To eat so ineptly, or to daintily nibble a bit held between thumb and forefinger, or to just sit there looking as though I wondered how to do it—whatever I tried was impolite.

I was making my twenty-seventh toss with no increase in skill, when I heard a knock at my door. It was Jon, my only Peace Corps Volunteer neighbor, whose post in Dhulikhel was only some five miles away. He had been giving a *bhoj* to which the guest of honor, who had demanded that he give this party, didn't come. He was annoyed about that, and furious that the key to his *charpi* had been stolen and the place fouled. And his strawberries had been stolen. We condoled with each other. I persuaded him to eat some of the cornbread I'd baked in an aluminum pan over my kerosene burner, and a mango compote, which we ate with spoons. I had gladly washed my hands and abandoned my practice at Nepali eating.

Jon came to Nepal in the Peace Corps group after mine. He was an architectural student one year out of college. He had great enthusiasm and a fine capacity for friendship. We saved each other's sanity on a number of occasions.

This time he had brought his sleeping bag and come over to spend the night in my second-floor sitting room because he had to have his measuring tape, which an official of Banepa had borrowed and failed to return as he'd promised. Jon had waited for him until the last bus, and then had to walk the five miles to my place to try to catch him in the morning.

Jon's job was overseer, working for the Dhulikhel *Panchayat* (governing committee of five). His group, he told me, had recently met and decided to tell the Peace Corps not to send any more overseers. It was not a viable job, they thought. To be useful and satisfactory to both sides it would have taken adjustment and understanding from both American and Nepali, almost always impossible to reach in a year or two.

The whole village of Dhulikhel seemed to love Jon, and he gave them his time unstintingly, enjoying it much of the time, but driven often to frustration. Dhulikhel was a much lovelier village than Banepa. From its *tundikhel* (the parade ground), the view of the Himalayas was superb. It was a prize place to bring tourists for a look at what they always wanted to see: Everest.

I used to go over frequently to watch the sunset while drinking (after my hepatitis had subsided) a glass of Three Tigers whiskey with Jon. This was a poisonous-tasting Nepali whiskey, but more palatable than *raksi*, the local distillate. We would sit and unwind from the day's work and watch the mountains laid out in hundreds of miles of display before us. In the beginning they would be white, with blue shadows on the snows. Some days we could hardly tell which was cloud, which mountain, except for the angles of their outlines. We would watch the changing shades as the sun set, and we would talk about everything—life at home, life in Nepal, our faraway families, the lives we used to lead, and how we felt about the present strange one. An outpouring of all the things it would have been impossible to speak about to anyone else. No other Americans lived as we Peace Corps Volunteers did, in the midst of Nepalis, holding the same jobs as they, living in houses built for ordinary people. Other Americans lived in compounds with servants and gardens as buffers. They had cars and access to the American PX. At the other end of the scale were American hippies; but they held no jobs, were not integrated into Nepali life as we were. Our lives and problems were unique.

Jon had met a shaman and we wanted to have a session with him. We missed him one evening but found him next morning, and Jon begged his services on my behalf. The shaman and his father, a bent old man with a huge tumor on one cheek, both wore shirt, vest, and *dhoti-suruwal*, much patched and not very clean. His father was his assistant. He agreed to help me and asked for oil, rice, red powder, water, string, and twisted wicks. I gave his old father some money, and while he went to get the necessary things, the shaman told us his story.

From the beginning he was set apart. Only boys who had 30 special characteristics were taken by the jungle shaman as he was taken one night in his sleep. His mother and father looked for him for days but could not find him. The shaman took him up a high cliff. Terrified, he hung on by his fingernails trying to keep up with his mysterious guide. Suddenly a door opened in the cliff showing a courtyard and house inside. He looked around for the shaman, but found he had turned into an earthworm. The boy stayed there for a time he could not estimate, learning to be a shaman, memorizing mantras, chants, medicines and ancient lore of all kinds.

At this point in his story he stopped talking and began to hum or buzz under his breath. He stood up and held a pleated white cheesecloth skirt up toward the flame his father had lit. He tied it around his waist. Sanctifying the rest of his costume the same way, he put beads around his neck and at his wrists, and twisted a red-and-white cloth around his head, buzzing steadily. Now he picked up his drum. More rituals of decorating it with bottle brush flowers, bowing to it, touching it with red powder. He asked for *raksi*, but instead of drinking it, he dipped the drumstick into the glass and sprinkled it around himself and us. Bells rang and incense filled the air. By now quite a crowd had come into the room to watch.

He began to chant softly. Calling on the gods—Bara Devi, Chara Devi, Shiva Ram, something about a door and all the little gods. His chant and the drum grew louder. He commenced bouncing as he sat crosslegged. Faster and faster. His eyes were blind. His arm was muscular and tense. His whole body was rigid. He bounced higher and higher. The spirit spoke through his lips quite differently from his own voice.

I had asked for news of my sons who were far away. The spirit voice began by telling me that I had three sons, which was correct. It paused and the shaman bounced harder, his eyes nearly closed. The assistant waved the oil lamp he had lit at the beginning, threw some rice toward it. The voice went on, coming strangely from the lips of the entranced shaman. "Your eldest son is about to be married. Your second son is very happy and is about to have a son." A long pause while his eyelids quivered. "Your youngest son is in China."

"No," I said.

"Your youngest son is in some country we do not know."

I could see that this was most likely true. My son was in Israel, from which all the ancient gods had been driven out by Jehovah so long ago that the country had been lost to memory in the world of spirits and enchantment.

The shaman bounced more quietly and the father handed him a small piece of paper. On it he placed rice, and some leaves he took out of his garments. He made marks with his fingernail on the paper and folded it into a tiny packet, chanting what were obviously special words, a charm. He tied it into a many-times-wrapped bundle and handed it to me.

He became quiet and sat entranced for a few moments. Then in his natural voice he asked me, "Was the spirit right?" "I think so; I did not know about the new baby." He smiled.

Jon and I had another encounter with shamans. This time they were *jhankris* of the hill people, who were moving from all the mountain villages along high trails toward Nagarkot, where a great religious festival would take place. During the day *jhankris* in long white skirts and high peacock-feather headdresses had been passing through Banepa toward the Shiva sanctuary and sacred pool on the mountain top at Nagarkot.

"Should we try to follow them?" asked Jon, but it was raining and I could visualize those trails. I temporized.

However, next morning I was wakened at 5:15 by the sound of a crackling fire. From my high kitchen window I could see that a water buffalo was being singed in Dilip's courtyard. Obviously a great feast was coming, though I didn't know what. It would have nothing to do with the *jhankris*, who were the shamans of the hill people, but I was awake and having second thoughts. The rain had stopped. If Jon wanted to go to Nagarkot, I would too. I went out to see if the goat-meat seller had arrived and if I could buy a heart. It would make fine sandwiches in the bread I had carried back on the bus from Kathmandu the day before yesterday. The butcher sat cross-legged at his corner and I came back with the heart wrapped in a big green leaf. I had almost missed Jon. I found him turning away from my door. We quickly cooked the heart, made and ate French toast, sliced the heart and bread for sandwiches, using canned butter, also from Kathmandu. We started west up the bazaar.

It was lovely for the first hour-and-a-half on the easy trail to Nala, a town famous for its three-story pagoda. Then, just as the trail steepened, it began to get hot. We passed some thatch-roofed houses, went through a little wood, then north over a saddle. We began to see many pilgrims on the trail, but we were late. Most going to Nagarkot were already there. These were coming from a new *Mahadev Pokhri* started last year. I had been there when it was initiated and regretted having missed it this year. There were always wonderful rituals going on that I only glimpsed, or never got to, or didn't even know existed. On we pressed to Nagarkot, even if we were late.

Just beyond the saddle was an improvised *raksi* shop of bamboo and some inebriated men who tried to delay us. We exchanged remarks, but kept on going. Upward we went across bare land. A tree where we wanted to rest looked to be a minute away but took us twelve to reach. At its foot we found a small thatched shrine built over a numinous stone. The god in the stone had been worshipped that morning. It was daubed with fresh red powder, and two dahlia heads lay upon it. Here we sat to eat some of our lunch though it was only 11:30.

We had been talking constantly when the slope did not take all our breath. Here on the broad saddle a vast view of Kathmandu valley opened before us. Behind us our own valley was closer and more beautiful with its dark hills, brilliant green paddy terraces, and silver rivers. We gazed for a time, then turned to the little shrine beside us. Jon made a gesture of respect and picked some leaves to put on the stone. "We're on a pilgrimage. We must pay our respects to all the gods we pass," he said, and I added a piece of bread. He looked hard at the stone. "I wonder what god this is?" After a while he asked, "Do people discover gods, or invent them?"

I said, "Remember the story about the tree that fell in the forest? The one that crashed silently because there was no ear to hear it fall? Maybe the primeval gods were like that. Perhaps they roamed the ancient world for eons waiting for humans to come and call them into being and worship them."

Inevitably a group of Nepalis stopped to stare at us and block our view. Onward and upward we went, swearing gaspingly that we would never climb again. Nagarkot was 3,500 feet higher than the 4,500 foot altitude of Banepa, and the round trip was 15 miles. About noon the first *jhankri* came down, dancing by us with his drummer and his followers. The women of his party were in brightly colored saris and wore all their fortune in gold jewelry. They stopped to perform for us since we had missed them at the top. The drummer drummed, the *jhankri* threw his spirit dagger at the ground and danced around it, chanting. He had a fine face and performed a wonderful ceremony for us. A couple of children started shrilling about money, asking exorbitant fees. I looked around for the *jhankri*'s wife, but couldn't see her in the crowd. After a bit she came up to me and put her arms around me, saying proudly to me, with a look at the jhankri, "My husband." I gave her the money I had ready and my best smile of appreciation. There is no word for thank you in Nepali. (Foreigners sometimes say *dhayabad* but Nepalis don't use it.)

Soon we reached the jeep road that wound along the crest— hurrying now, not to miss all the rest. Just ahead was the Pool of Shiva. It was, perhaps, a hundred feet across. Many people were still taking ritual baths, the men in loincloths, the women bare to the waist. I remembered Jnan Kaji saying to me, "Isn't it beautiful?" as we watched another ceremonial bathing. On one bank several *jhankris* were finishing their ceremonious performances. We went first to a Shiva *lingam* in an enclosure of fresh boughs. The priest motioned me to come ahead so I bowed and placed some money on the *lingam*. He gave me a red *tika* mark on my forehead. So did the priest at our next stop, a small prostrate Mahadev statue above the spring that fed the pool.

All the *jhankris* had finished and gone by this time except a very young one, whose drummers were women. We watched him until he, too, put away his spirit knife and horn, and, still dancing, started on a downward trail. Jon had talked about a rest or a nap before we went home, but we started right off. A friendly man whose village was above Nala showed us a new way down and we followed him, winding around the contour of the hill, forever it seemed, after a few sharp slippery descents. When he saw Jon offer me his hand at a difficult spot, our guide started doing it, too.

Once we sighted two water buffaloes below us in a stream. Hoping for enough water to swim in, we hurried down, but there was hardly a pool. The buffaloes were gone. We sat and dangled our legs in the heavenly cool water just above a small waterfall. All around us were tiny purple iris.

While we cooled our feet I told Jon the history of Kavre College that Ram Bhakta had told me of so proudly a few months earlier. They did start it as a late afternoon college in the Ajad High School building. I was asked to teach a class in English composition. I began by assigning Kamala Markandaya's charming *Nectar in a Sieve* to read as a basis for our first discussion. I got the books from Kathmandu for them but immediately it was apparent that none of the 20 students in the class was able to read it. I tried again, asking them to study *Peter Rabbit*. That was better. We began to talk about what makes a story. Two of them grasped some of the essentials; the others were interested and were beginning to understand, but at that point the authorities in Kathmandu ordered the college closed. It did not come up to the standards they were just setting for a college.

"Poor Banepa," said Jon, "It sounds just like some of the projects our *Panchayat* talks about starting."

We followed along our path through the jungle until it led us, just above Nala, to a marvelous view centered by the golden three-tiered temple, the tile roofs of the town, and a nearby pool of another temple. One more steep bit of trail and then the level slog home. Coming into Banepa, we saw my neighbor the priest reading to a big group of children under a shelter of poles and straw. Without pausing in his story from the *Ramayana,* he gave me his wonderful smile as we passed. We stopped a second to say "*Namaste*" to Ram Bhakta, Gobinda, and Asa Kaji when we saw them sitting in their neighborhood tea house. Ram Bhakta insisted on taking us next door to his home and giving us some fresh corn from their *khet* and a couple of *chapattis* with some of his mother's jam made after the recipe I had taught her. She and the children were proud of it. We were too tired, but they were all so hospitable we couldn't refuse. Back to my place. One drink with Jon before he started back to Dhulikhel. Then I ate a tiny banana and went to bed at 8:30.

There were wonderful days of trekking to a village I didn't know, where Jon was helping the villagers build a coulee to bring water two miles closer. There were evenings of talk that helped to assuage the loneliness I was almost willing to admit now to myself.

Before, I felt my hurt was too violent to be called grief or loneliness. Now it had become a settled ache that flared often into deeper pain and desperation. The ache never left, but I knew now I was lonely for someone of my own kind. A loneliness separate from grief.

I would sit of an evening and say to myself, "I don't want to climb the hill again to look at the sunset. I don't want to go out and sit crosslegged on the ground to talk with Krishna Maya and the other women in the court. I don't want to go see Krishna Prasad. I don't want to meet a special visitor they have up at the Adventist Hospital. I just want somebody who sees life more or less the way I do, to drop by for a bit of conversation." That was the void Jon stepped into. No one who has not known long periods of isolation from whatever means home to him, can completely understand what a friend is.

22

Up To the Mountains

D ASAIN WAS THE GREATEST FESTIVAL of the year,
but I never saw it in Banepa. It began about the first of
October. After the rains had ceased and the harvest was
gathered the whole country rejoiced in ten days of celebration.

His Majesty's Government went on holiday. Schools closed.
Nepalis went back to their home villages. Some of them walked
many days to reach the place where they must spend this very
holy and joyful time with their families. Foreigners went on
trek to the mountains. I could hardly wait to be off to see more
of this marvelous land.

When my first Dasain arrived, I was just over an eight-
month bout with hepatitis. I was not going to ask anyone to
slow his pace to mine, but I was determined to try trekking,
though I had never done anything like it in my life. Ted, the
very tall boy in our Nepal 18 group, was a great trekker by now.
He had begun practice early—it was three days' hard walk
before he even reached his village. Ted and I ran into each other
in Kathmandu about this time. He seemed to have it arranged
that Bill, the librarian of our group, and I should trek together.
Bill swore that he was a slow walker and really wanted to go
with me.

For advice and help in this activity, so new and strange to me,
I went to Jimmy Roberts, a former Major of Ghurkhas and
founder of the now-famous Mountain Travel. He just said,
"You are a Peace Corps Volunteer. You don't need any help
from me." Put thus on my mettle, I went to the proper
government office for a trekking permit, and to Third Eye
Travel for a plane ticket to Pokhara, the starting place for our
trek. After several days of delay and contretemps, I got a ticket.

(I saw His Majesty King Mahendra wandering around the airport one day. Even he was having trouble getting a plane.) I hired a porter. Bill was going to carry his own pack. We couldn't get tickets on the same day, so I flew to Pokhara to wait. The plane was a two-engine job with benches along the sides and baggage piled all down the center. The pilot sent a message inviting me to sit in the co-pilot's seat where the view was stupendous. I longed for Howard to share it.

When the people on the ground at Pokhara saw the plane coming they blew a loud whistle to warn the owners of all the cattle, buffaloes, and goats to get their beasts off the field. From the plane I could see a dozen or so being hurried to safety. But in Pokhara it is hard to look at anything except the towering mountains, brilliantly filling the northern sky.

Next afternoon, October 13, rather late, Bill arrived. Also my porter. We wasted more time while he tried to buy me a big black umbrella in the bazaar. A taxi took us through town on the last bit of road between us and Tibet. There we started on a trail used long before history was written.

Our destination was Jomosom, as far to the north as our trekking permit would allow us to go. Just writing about trekking makes my heart beat faster. Even now, years later, I remember most of the steps of that trail. It starts gently along a river. We stopped at the Tibetan camp for tea from Tibetans who had fled from the Chinese invasion of their country. Then on across the Mardi Khola River on a bamboo bridge. All along this part of the trail were scattered huts, some of them with painted designs on red ochre walls. With *jholas* slung over our shoulders and umbrellas furled, we walked across a great grassy space at Hyangia, and almost flat fields to Suikhet. To the north Machhapuchhare and the Annapurnas travelled with us.

While we were crossing the fields we had a little adventure. A group of horsemen came riding toward us, the only people we ever saw riding. Horses, here, were pack animals. The leader wore what looked like a shallow brass bowl on his head, very shiny and somehow impressive. His retinue wore embroidered headcloths. The horses jingled with innumerable bells. The leader hailed us and stopped to chat about how things were in Kathmandu. We found out later he was the Rajah of the lost Tibetan kingdom of Mustang. His bowl must have been his gold crown. The lady riding sidesaddle was the Rani.

Suikhet was a hamlet with a *buttee*, a hut where we bought *bhat*, little fish, vegetable curry, and pickles for 4 rupees (40 cents)—and also a place to stretch out on the floor, for another 2 rupees. In most *buttees* very little stretching was possible. I had a thin roll of foam rubber and a down sleeping bag, inside which I dressed and undressed.

The woman who cooked our food wore ten gold loops around the periphery of each ear, a big gold stud through the center of her ear, a smaller one through the little tab of flesh at the front, a huge one in the earlobe, and a nose stud. What surprised me was that she later slept with all this wealth firmly in place. There were two men carrying laden *dhokas*, and three mule drivers sleeping there that night. Also a man and his porter we were to meet again. A German from Berlin.

The next morning, after eggs and tea, and a couple of bananas l had brought with me, Bill and I left Suikhet and began to climb. The worst part was 1,000 feet up a rough stairway of jumbled rocks. To our unaccustomed legs and hearts it was severe. Pokhara is at an altitude of 2,572 feet, Suikhet 3,100, Naudanda 4,782. Strange birds flew in trees covered with orchids. From then on no two steps were ever on the level. Everything was up or down. My right knee hurt, the one with the old injury. But I got up quite handily to the top of that first climb and the hamlet of Naudanda with a view to stir your heart. Across a deep valley with several villages of oval huts were four peaks of Annapurna, each one over 26,000 feet, and in front of them, looking higher than its 24,000 feet was Machhapuchhare, the Fishtail, a sharply steep and spectacular peak.

They seemed much closer here and more impressive. The Everlasting Hills, so quickly changing in geologic time, the newest hills of all, these great ones, with the shells of oceans lying on them, lifted up slowly from the ocean bottom to the top of the world. We humans come and go in a second, but that second is so full of passionate joy and anguish. How many different lives have passed as these mountains rose? Here am I, protoplasm clad in rubber, cotton, leather and wool. With a metal-topped and cloth-covered stick in my hand. Drinking tea and eating the eggs of a feathered flying animal whose like was not in the world as these mountains began to be pushed up. Here am I with delight and amazement in my heart and words to try to express it. What will the creature be like who sees Machhapuchhare as a grassy knoll worn down again by the ages?

In Naudanda the houses are stone and thatch. From the upstairs room at the *buttee* where we had tea, you can look out the back window at the great valley of the Harpen Khola to the big lake, Phewa Tal, above the airfield. It was our last glimpse of "civilization."

Though neither Bill nor I would ever be outstanding trekkers, we learned gradually that it was best to keep plodding uphill, no matter how slowly, without stopping till we came to a dip in the trail. We carried big black old-fashioned umbrellas. There was not much chance of rain, now that monsoon was over, but they were a shelter from the sun. Alternately, we could slide them through the strap of the *jholas* carried over our shoulders, holding the galling strap in a different position. We could almost lean on the furled umbrella as we struggled upward. Each of us had to go at his own pace; sometimes we met for a bar of chocolate when one of us caught up with the other resting.

After Naudanda the trail went along a ridge and we could see both valleys, could look back to distant Pokhara and to Suikhet. Below us were a square stone temple on a hill, and a big pond where water buffaloes were submerging themselves. People passed dressed in bright new clothes, and with huge red *tikas* of *bhat* on their foreheads. (These were for the Dasain rituals, as were the ferris-wheel-like swing we saw in one village, and the buffalo being slaughtered ritually in another.)

The man from Berlin toiled up beside me. It was nice to find someone going almost as slowly as I was. He was Herr Mettich, a retired engineer who had started a technical school in Syria. We stepped aside for a flock of sheep with curled horns, led by a few twisty-horned goats, their horns or coats marked in gay colors for identification. They were on their way to Kathmandu to become lamb curries.

After the pass at Khare (three houses) we went down the valley of a river unnamed on our map. Rice terraces, rushing streams. Always down now. We stopped for tea in Chandrakot where there is a magnificent pipal tree in the middle of a stone platform, arranged here, as rests are all along the trail, so a person with a loaded *dhoka* can sit and rest the basket on a shelf at just the right level to take the load off his tired shoulders. Most of the men, women, and children we met were carrying *dhokas*, including women in velvet blouses. My own goods were in one on Gunga Bahadur's back. A little girl walked with me, carrying a few corn cobs in her *dhoka*. Her brother, who came back up the trail to get her, had a pot of sweet custard in his.

Here at Chandrakot, after a day of walking, we had rounded Machhapuchhare far enough to see the twin points of the fishtail for which it is named. It stood far to the north up the Modi Khola gorge. To the south the river cut through a series of hills and mountains on its way toward the great Ganges. East lay the valley and ridge we had traversed: to the west the Bharungi Valley led up the way we must go the next day. Below us, about 1,500 feet below, gleamed the slate roofs of Birethanti, shining in the sun where two white foaming rivers converged.

At 4:30. I was getting tired. I had come down straight for an hour and the end was not in sight. A tethered water buffalo, in a shed beside the rock I sat on, chewed his cud. Beyond him

was a picture in blue and white—Annapurna framed in cloud
and sky. After a while I stood up and went on down. Mahonia
and bauhinia (if that is the name of the orchid-flowered tree)
grew along the trail. A small bright-eyed Nepali woman caught
up with me and slowed down to talk. She asked about my children and all the usual questions. When she decided she must go
on, she merely walked down the trail away from me, disappear-
ing round the next bend in a minute or two. I ran to try to keep
up with her graceful walk, but it was no good. She was gone.

Dhoka. Author feared having to be carried in a *dhoka* like this man.

In a minute a young boy joined me. He is Chandra Bahadur Magar, sixth class in school. His father is dead, his brother a non-com in the British Army. "What would you do, Chandra Bahadur, if you had 100 rupees?" "I would go to *Belait* (England)."

Down at last to a sturdy bridge across the river. I waited for another herd of sheep to be driven across, and Herr Mettich joined me. Bill was already in Birethanti, across the bridge. He had found us a rather good *buttee*. That night Herr Mettich showed us his old Leica camera and told us it had been buried in his Berlin back yard in 1939 for safe keeping and dug up after the war was over.

He confided to us that he had a special reason for coming to Nepal. He wanted to meet Gurkha soldiers in the hope that he would find some who had fought against the Germans at Monte Casino. Those brave little enemies had fought so courageously against him that he had always hoped he could know them in peace. At every hamlet he asked for Gurkha soldiers, because it was from the Gurungs and Magars of these villages that many of the Gurkha regiments had come.

I hadn't slept the first night and was tired. Now there were beds! Everyone else seemed to be using their pillows, so after crawling into my sleeping bag I gratefully rested my head on mine. During the night I felt as though tiny things were jumping softly onto my face. A week later I would find out I hadn't been dreaming.

Early in the morning I walked a way up the river and bathed in the cold fresh water. Beside me a little white-breasted gray bird, a dipper, walked underwater on the river bottom in the amazing way his species can.

On the trail again, we met Mike, another of our Peace Corps group. He was seven days out and suffering from a bad knee, but going fast and enjoying it still. He gave us good advice and glowing stories about the rest of our route.

All day up the valley. A morning stop for tea at Tirkkhe

Dinga. Chickens running in and out. Delicious-smelling mushrooms cooking. Gunga Bahadur gossips with Didi, the big sister of the house. A little girl by the door (the only light source) is reciting and writing first grade arithmetic. She is wearing gold earrings and nose ring. Her baby brother has gold bracelets. The fire is at the back of the room. There is one small pot only, and a three-legged iron stand for it. A shaped stone and a stone pestle for grinding grain, and a flat metal sheet for frying *chapattis*. That is all. Under the eaves a chicken in a basket is laying an egg. Outside a mule train is assembling with much jingling of harness and bells.

We crossed the river and began to climb more steeply. By about 2:30 my bad knee was swollen and giving me real pain. An Ace bandage and lanosil from Bill and Herr Mettich seemed to help. It took to 4:00 to get to Ulleri, less than halfway to the pass from the last bridge. I was slow, every step hurt, but neither of our two porters was willing to go any faster up this very steep trail anyway. An eagle soared far above us. Flowering almond trees were in bloom. We reached Ulleri and found a house where we could stay for the night.

Next day, October 17, my knee is still bad and I don't want to go on. Ahead is the pass at Ghorpani, about 9,000 feet. From there it is 4,000 feet or so down to the Kali Ghandaki River, and that much farther from any medical help. The only way for one who cannot walk is to be carried in a *dhoka*. I urge Bill to go on. "I'll be all right. There is another Peace Corps couple behind us. Please, Bill, go ahead with them." He won't. He insists that if he had sprained his ankle I wouldn't have left him. "We came as equals," he says. "I won't desert you."

So I stay in Ulleri to rest a day. He goes on up to Ghorpani with Herr Mettich to get a look at Dhaulagiri across the next valley. Right now six very dirty children who've obviously *never* had their noses wiped clean are standing close to watch me write. A big child sits beside me. Ulleri is a Magar village. Its oval houses, stuccoed with mud, are thatched and have smoke holes at the two gabled ends. I should sleep. Last night there were very strange noises, then talking and flash-light play for hours. I was somewhat frightened.

I sit on the narrow terrace in front of the house. Below among the houses I see the same topiary trees of corn drying in the husks that were at Yegya's house. Hawks sail in the valley far below. Musical bells of mule trains ring as they go down over the steep steps of the trail. Most mules wear colorful crests and ornaments. Saddle blankets are hand-woven Tibetan rugs. Small triangular woven forehead ornaments, woven dyed halters, and red pom-poms show the owner's pride in his mule. Holes in a couple of saddle bags full of rice are plastered shut with dung.

In the morning we start down. Two days' lodging and food was 11 rupees ($1.10). Seven goats descend the zig-zag trail through the village ahead of us. We make it down the mountain in an hour and a half. Knee not bad. You must place your foot sidewise on a lot of the rocks of this rough stair-like trail.

When I got back to Kathmandu the Peace Corps Doctor told me I could have taken aspirin and gone on. He also found that I had lice. They turned out to be a terrible pest to get rid of. I gave myself a germicidal shampoo, and left my disinfected clothes outdoors for 24 hours. The Peace Corps Doctor even had his Nepali maid go over my head with a fine-toothed comb looking for nits. I stayed in Kathmandu at the Shankar Hotel where many international officials stayed in those days. I got my hair done. I wore my pink dress. That evening I looked around the room glittering under chandeliers and thought to myself, "I am the best looking woman in the room. And nobody suspects I have lice!"

23

Trying Again

A YEAR AND A HALF LATER, in January, I tried the same trek again (having gotten a little more experience in the Everest region in the meantime). I got all the way to Jomosom that time, somewhat redeeming myself in my own eyes. I took with me my sister and brother-in-law, Rosamond and Russell. He had finished some work in India, and they came to Nepal to visit me. Again we had to fly on separate planes, but this time the planes arrived within ten minutes of each other, which had one strange little consequence.

A young couple, Marilyn and Bill Kopp, had been talking to Rose and Russ in the Kathmandu airport, but didn't know they were with me. The plane was unloading. They were retrieving their new red backpacks, when they saw the porters I'd arranged for, meeting us and loading gear into a taxi. I heard Bill saying to Marilyn, "We made a mistake. They aren't our kind of people at all."

It didn't make me feel effete to take a taxi for the first two miles, and I would readily admit that I needed a porter, but I could see how they looked down on us.

Rose and Russ were better trekkers than I. We sailed along the part of the trail I knew, stopping in Ulleri three days later and continuing up toward the pass above Ghorpani. It was still a long steep climb, and my brother-in-law had begun to feel sick and had to go slowly. Nevertheless we all made it to the camp just below the pass that night.

183

It was hard. I tried to stay back with them, but found, as I had learned before, that my endurance gives out about four o'clock. Too late, I began to walk ahead at my own pace. I saw them far below me on the trail, then lost them at a curve and was all alone. Our porters were somewhere above. I felt exhausted and decided I must lie down for few a minutes of rest. But, as I picked a mossy bank and sank down on it, I saw the sun was going to set in a few minutes and I would lose all its heat. By now I was so exhausted that my mind had stopped working very well. I got up and walked up the trail about 100 feet to make the sun set a little later, before I lay down again. Luckily for me, as I lowered myself I saw, only 300 feet ahead, the huts of our stopping place with smoke pouring out through the flimsy roofs.

Rose and Russ got there hours later exhausted, but next morning we were all enchanted by the forest around the pass, a forest of rhododendron trees 30 feet tall, hung with garlands of moss and inhabited by leaping gray langur monkeys. There was a little snow on the ground, but our barefoot porters strode ahead disregarding it. At the pass itself we had our first sight of the majesty of Dhaulagiri. But even downhill, Russ felt worse and worse. About three o'clock we stopped for the night at Sikha.

We set up the tent Rose and Russ slept in beside the house where I planned to stay. Russ lay down to rest. Rose and I sat on the wall outside, just above the trail. Along came two trekkers with red backpacks. They looked up and saw Rose and me. Their mouths flew open in amazement. How could these effete, soft, middle-aged people be ahead of them on the trail? Impossible! their faces said. We greeted Marilyn and Bill Kopp nicely, and only crowed a bit to each other after they left.

That afternoon I visited a school beside a little temple. The children were sitting on the ground, wrapped in shawls. On a small standing blackboard the young male teacher had drawn a picture of the temple. Under it was printed the word *mandir* in Nepali script. While the huddled children wrote on their slates, the teacher and I discussed teaching methods. Across the valley Dhaulagiri's snows were beginning to be tinged with pink. Great gashes above us on our forested mountain showed where large pieces of it had slid. The peasants burn the grass and bushes under the trees to make better pasture, but this weakens the cover and makes landslides worse in this steep new land.

I turned west again toward the glory of Dhaulagiri. The pink was deepening, but cloud was forming on its lower slopes and drifting over the shoulder of its neighbor, Tukche Peak. The clouds thickened and thinned. Thickened again, rising all the time, veiling then revealing the two, now almost peach-colored, peaks. I watched, mesmerized. Constantly the clouds were changing and I seemed to see the mountains shifting behind the whirls of mist. They were turning white again, cold. They settled down firmly on the earth. I opened my eyes wider. Had they been flying for a second or two?

Next morning we made it down to the Kali Gandaki River, where we crossed on the bridge shown on Toni Hagen's book cover, the perilous bridge I'd stared at before leaving for Peace Corps training. It was rebuilt now and solid. Then upstream to Tato Pani, where hot springs filled a square pool, and drifts of steam escaped between the rocks of the river shore. Here Russ and Rose set up their tent in an orange grove of a wealthy family, who took me into the house to sleep in my sleeping bag. What heaven Tato Pani was! Hot water to sink gratefully into, lemons and oranges to eat. We had had nothing but *dal-bhat* and biscuit. An egg when one was available. Here poinsettias 12 feet tall bloomed against the view of Nilgiri with its steep rocks and snow.

Russ felt feverish to my hand, but kept saying he would be all right. However, we found a trekking doctor with a thermometer, and Russ's temperature was 102. I had tetracycline with me, and he began on the prescribed course. Next morning he felt too ill to go on, but he and Rose insisted I leave them there.

Finally persuaded, I left them all my tetracycline and pushed ahead with one porter, Min Bahadur.

We were in Dana in one-and-a-half hours, a half-hour ahead of the schedule on my trekking map. Here was the first check point where I must stop to have my trekking permit stamped. The trail was a slow, continuing upgrade. Our eleven o'clock *bhat* stop was beside wonderful Ruchchara waterfall, where there were three *buttees* with mats for walls and roofs. White Annapurna just showed through the cut to the South. We went on. A bridge and then a sharp turn into a sheer black rock wall, beside a steep canyon. Up and up. Hot work. Then down to the gravelled river bed and along it toward Ghasa. A parklike stretch with a wide sand road between stone walls lined with feathery bamboo. Big pines and steep slopes on both sides. A steep bluff rises above Ghasa.

Min Bahadur refused to go on to the next town though it was only 3:30 in the afternoon. Our stop allowed me time to explore the town with its flat-roofed stone houses. Footholds scooped in logs made ladders to the useful space on top stacked with wood and straw. I watched men bringing in big *dhoka* loads of pine needles which they strewed on the one street. A stream was channeled through the town beside it. Pretty, friendly children greeted me as I passed. They weren't begging in those days as they do now that so many trekkers pass and give them money or presents.

I wandered up toward the high cliff I'd seen from the trail. It was there that I found my little water-wheel made from a turnip. At the foot of a beautiful waterfall, in a small side-stream beside a tiny shrine, something was moving. The bit of red cloth, at the top of the spindle stuck through the turnip, was whirling busily round and round, sending up its tiny prayers to the gods. A black and white fantail scraped and hopped under willow branches overhanging the streamlet.

My *buttee* was evidently a yak stop. There were ten yaks in the yard and shed when I came back. More than a dozen yak drivers and owners came in to eat, a few at a time. Most of these animals are crossbred with cows, not full-blooded yaks. I found it difficult to understand the names that they used for the males and females. I asked to have them written for me in Nepali but no one could write. Finally the mother, who was cooking for us, pushed a little girl forward. She was in third grade, the only literate person there.

After everyone was through eating, while the mother spun goat's wool, the little girl helped her twelve-year-old sister wash the dishes, and do one last sweeping of the one-room house. (It was the twelve-year-old who was first up in the morning to lay the fire and mud the floor.) I spread my sleeping bag and looked up at the square hole cut in the ceiling above the central fire. I slept in my clothes and put my shoes inside the sleeping bag with me to keep them warm for morning. I had told Min Bahadur we would go to Marpha tomorrow, from there to Jomosom and back the next day. He agreed.

But I found he had been right when he stopped us the day before. The trail to the next village, Lete, was very difficult and steep. Small puddles were frozen. Even in our morning freshness we didn't reach it till our regular eleven o'clock stopping time although we had started at seven. We sat around an open fire to eat with the villagers. They kept asking me questions and repeating all my answers to each other. I felt like a cute baby. Look, she can talk!

Down again to the wide, rubble-strewn bed of the Kali Gandaki. Sometimes the trail was cut into the rock of the bank, very narrow, hardly room to squeeze along above scary sheer drops to the bottom.

By the time we got to Tukche (another check point where I must get my permit stamped) we were in Buddhist country. It was a pretty town of stone houses with beautifully carved balconies and ochre-painted arches leading into courtyards full of yaks and goats. The trekking official here was an obliging man who let me use a room of his house to change to my longjohns. Beyond was Marpha, in one of whose stone houses I stayed in a room by myself. Beyond it again, was Jomosom, at the end of a strange barren landscape. From here on the trail was forbidden to foreigners.

As I headed for the end, Marilyn and Bill caught up with me and we walked together. They had left their red packs in Marpha since we had to go back through it. They were planning on the return trip to climb up to the glacier above Kobang and invited me to go with them. I hated to say no, but I had to get back to my sister and her husband.

There wasn't much to Jomosom. We got out our trekking permits before turning back, but when Bill pulled theirs from his pocket he found he'd brought another folder by mistake. The permit was back in Marpha. The official said he must stamp it. He was adamant, and our attempts at persuasion, as well as my try at bribery in my best Nepali, didn't move him. Bill must walk back two hours to Marpha to get it. Four hours lost. The officer would keep Marilyn as a hostage to be sure he returned. Again we pled and stormed and offered money, but he would not yield. So, poor Bill went back as fast as he could. We met just before I got to Marpha and shared a couple of my chocolate bars in forlorn celebration of having reached Jomosom.

That night I was back in Kobang, on a little promontory stretching out into the Kali Gandaki. Annapurna towered more than 26,000 feet above me on one side and Dhaulagiri at the same altitude faced it across what is said to be the deepest gorge in the world. Their two peaks were only 25 miles apart. From Tukche Peak beside Dhaulagiri a glacier hung over the town of Kobang and its temples.

It was a magic night. First the sun set over Dhaulagiri, staining the snows of Annapurna rose. The glacier hanging over us was a paler pink. At 5:30 a full disk of silver-gilt slowly lifted out of the snows of Annapurna. By 5:40 all color was gone from the west and the full moonlight glittered on the ice fields of Dhaulagiri and Tukche and Annapurna, filling the sky with splendor. The earth made a foil for it, a great gray expanse of river rubble, dark pine and fir forest. On the tip of the rock point stood the silhouette of a temple, its finial pointed at the brilliant sky.

I kept getting up all night, putting on my down jacket, and going out to look at the glory. Once there was a dog howling with his muzzle to the sky on the roof of the next house. He had climbed the notched log ladder to get closer to it all.

24

Down From the Mountains

U NTIL CLOSE TO THE END of my tour of duty my
supervisor was an American, but in accordance with
Peace Corps policy he was replaced by a Nepali, Massadi
Mallick. Massadi was a wise and kind man. One day he appeared
at Ajad High School to observe my teaching. I remember it
was a lesson in biology in tenth class, the highest grade in the
school. It roughly corresponded to the senior year in an
American high school. Tenth grade biology was of great importance to any pupil who wanted to go on to higher education, or
try for a government job. It was one of the subjects covered in
the School Leaving Certification exam, the vital SLC.

I was speaking in Nepali, but writing on the board the
English terms that the children must know for the exam.
Massadi listened intently for most of the period, then went off
to talk to the Headmaster and, I realized later, he listened to my
next class from outside to see how it went when he was not
present. Afterward he said to me, "I will not send another
teacher to Banepa unless I can send a strong one like you." I was
overwhelmed. So I was doing all right after all?

I was trying so hard to overcome the problems that plagued
me that I didn't see at first that he was there, also, to evaluate
the school and decide whether he would let them have another
teacher for the next year. Many schools were begging him for
science teachers.

The end of my tour approached. Finally the last class was
over. The last marvelous trek had been taken. The last goodbyes
to my Nepali friends said. Nepal 18, my Peace Corps group
whom I had seen only in quick passings when we met by chance

in Kathmandu, gathered (all that were left of us) for the first time since we had separated to go to our villages. Our termination conference would be at Darjeeling, the old British hill station in the eastern Himalayas of India. One of the boys stationed at Okledunga, in the east, walked four days to get there. Most of us met in Kathmandu and flew to Biratnagar, where one of the boys had spent his two years teaching science. Biratnagar is in the Terai, Nepal's lowland belt next to India. I immediately realized how lucky I had been. I could never have stood the heat of the Terai.

We crossed the Indian border and entrained for Bagdogra. There was a change of trains at midnight and the boarding of a third-class carriage because something had gone wrong with our second-class reservations. That something should have gone wrong was no surprise, but the third-class carriage was. There were three bare board shelves on each side of the compartments. It was so crowded that our men shoved us women on, and somehow caught on themselves as the train started moving. I was pushed aboard. Mike lifted his cello to me, and five Indians trying to climb up pushed me into a stinking open toilet with the cello in my arms. After he had jammed himself aboard and caught his breath, Jim rescued me and made a place on a second shelf for me. Below, above, and standing, in the compartment was a mass of humanity. I could see a few of my group, but all we could do was raise our eyebrows at each other and laugh. No one could move.

At Bagdogra we had breakfast in the station and shook ourselves several times for the joy of having room to do so. Then, instead of the wonderful single-gauge train that doubles back on itself as it winds up the mountain, we took the much quicker bus that reaches Darjeeling in eight hours.

I had visited there several times. Darjeeling was a delight to us in our joyful status of old-Nepal-hands because Nepali, not Hindi, is what you hear in the streets. When Peter walked in from Okledunga there were 19 of us left from the 72 who started training and the 46 who came to Nepal. One volunteer gave up before he ever reached his village, overtaken by the reality of the country—difficult trails, tiny thatch villages looking terribly primitive to someone straight from America. Twenty went home in the first few months. The Peace Corps paid their passage home, but they had to be back in the US in three days. No world wanderings on the way home. We lost more than the usual group of volunteers, having been tried more severely than most in some parts of our training and our reception in Nepal.

I looked at the ones who were left. They didn't look like the kids who had come out. These were men who had been on their own for two years, working against odds, making friends and a place for themselves, representing their country as they tried to help in this far corner of the world. It was just as true of the women, but there were only three of us left, only the older ones, Mary and I, and Rita who was about 30 and had been somewhat insulated in her job as secretary in the Medical Office in Kathmandu. Some of the stories the boys told showed ingenuity, and great understanding in the way they and their villagers worked together.

Ira had found one of the men of his village at the foot of a cliff, injured by falling. He picked him up and carried him three miles back to the village. In his Peace Corps kit he had disinfectant and aspirin. With these he treated the villager until he recovered. All the village came to him ever after for all their ills and wounds. They called him Doctor. Mike helped his villagers enlarge the school. Everyone had done something for *his village*. All of us had survived illnesses and strange difficulties that no one at home would believe, but here we all still, triumphantly, were.

Our moderator for the termination conference was the Assistant Director of Peace Corps, Thailand, a fine, level-headed young woman. She had moderated quite a number of termination conferences. No group of Peace Corps Volunteers she had ever met, she told us, loved their country the way we did. We knew its reality, but it was still a dream to us also. Not one of us but planned to come back. Not one of us was the same person who had arrived two years earlier. No one said it had been a piece of cake.

I looked at Mike, Ted, and Bruce, and Jim, and Bill. What a lot of new knowledge, and sympathy, and comprehension they were taking home with them. They were still only twenty-three or four. They had long lives ahead. Surely they would be a wonderful leaven in the American scene.

If we were ever able to sum up our two years of experiences I can't remember it. Perhaps we were still too close to them, but there was a yeast bubbling in all of us that would never allow our lives to be the same again, or our way of thought about the world and about other peoples. I still summed up the difference to myself as, "all the things everybody knows, just aren't so here." Bill quoted Isak Dinesen, "Their realities are not our realities." Kipling has been quoted too many times, but "the wildest dreams of Kew are (still) the facts of Kathmandu."

We had all learned something about ourselves, too. I think we all knew how impossible it is for any human to tear himself loose from his own culture—taken in with the "milk at his mother's breast"—enough to be completely objective about other people's beliefs. In myself I could recognize it in my feeling of pity about the waste of a life of the holy man who spent his days gazing at the great god Surje, the sun. Long years since, he had ruined the sight of his eyes. I couldn't help thinking how horrible it must be for him to one day realize what he had done to himself. It was years before I knew that such doubts would never have entered his devout soul. I found the same lack of comprehension in the perceptive and sensitive Fosco Mariani, traveler and student of Tibet. Even though he realized how tightly each one of us is bound by his own culture, he speculated that the little Tibetan Rimpoche, whom he knew well, must eventually be disillusioned. The young Rimpoche had been found by holy men to be a Bodhisatva who had renounced nirvana to be born again for the good of mankind. Taught so as a young child, and recognized as holy by his whole country, he naturally and simply accepted his own godhood. But Mariani thinks he must someday realize he is a hoax. Mariani is an Italian, and no Italian could be a god. However, a Tibetan could and the Rimpoche was one.

For me, though I didn't speak of it, there was a great sense of foreboding, as though I were already mourning the loss of a vital ancient way of life. I saw it still living but doomed in our modern world that we, I, all of us who meant so well, were helping to bring to Nepal. It was done at Nepali request, but it would change them and the country I loved, beyond recall.

At least in many ways we had learned, if not to think as a Nepali thinks, to feel and understand something of his reactions. We would carry always this understanding under our skins.

We had lived with the people, doing the same job our Nepali counterparts had. Heaven knows we had made mistakes, but we had been free from the feeling of superiority one of my English friends unknowingly expressed when she asked me, "But if you live like the Nepalis, do you find they respect you? Are they grateful for what you do for them?" Maybe not, but some of them loved us, and we loved them.

We would never have used the term elite for ourselves. But we were proud. We knew we were special. We had been set down in strange and difficult circumstances with a job to do, and we had done it. Each one had done it separately, all by himself. We looked at each other and saluted the brave moments we had lived through, each realizing the courage the others had shown.

Reluctantly, we bade farewell to our mountains, to our beautiful Nepal, to our frustrations and our triumphs. We headed down into ordinary life. For none of us would there ever again be a place or time like the one just ended.

Epilogue
Not Exactly An Answer

S O, HERE I AM, ready to go back home. Have I found an answer or even a palliative to the grief that drove me around the world to this land, now so dear to me?

No. I know, instead, that there will never be an answer. No matter what the rest of life holds for me, nothing will take the place of what is gone. But strangely I have found that I can live without that part of me. I can live with an unfilled and unfillable void inside my skin.

In recompense for my loss, there are three things I now possess:

A certain strength, as though the 33 years Howard and I had together were a kind of bulwark against whatever may come.

A knowledge of true loss and despair, and with this an ability to take lesser ills lightly. I have a gauge of what is serious, and what can be laughed at.

And I have a new area of the world to love and watch with affection and concern. My world has grown larger and more beautiful. Nepal is a treasure in my mind and heart.